Leadership in the Black Church:

Guidance in the Midst of Changing Demographics

By Dr. Michael Evans

Austin Brothers Publishing

Leadership in the Black Church
Guidance in the Midst of Changing Demographics

Published by Austin Brothers Publishing, Fort Worth, Texas

www.abpbooks.com

ISBN 978-0-9996328-2-6

Printed in the United States of America

2018 -- First Edition

I dedicate this work to the love of my life; my wife Lisa. Lisa has been the person I could depend on for support and encouragement. Early in our young lives, she sacrificed her career by agreeing to become my wife. She placed her college career on hold for a time to help me complete my undergraduate studies. My wife was my co-producer for our radio broadcast, The Truth, *that was taped in the living room of our one bedroom apartment. Lisa is the one who deserves the accolades for this book, along with my two sons Michael, Jr. and Richard Isaac. My family has sacrificed so much for the causes of which I believe I have been called. I pray that if one person is blessed by the words in this book, they will know one of the strong pillars of support that made this effort possible was my loving family and the unction of the Holy Spirit.*

ACKNOWLEDGMENTS

This work was made possible by hundreds of people God has placed in my life who were instrumental in the process of molding me as a servant and a man. It was the call of God upon my life that served as the driving force behind my ministerial efforts. Through His divine call, people poured into me the desire to seek an understanding of the true character and conduct of a servant-leader.

One example is my great grandmother who taught the importance of caring for people less fortunate. She demonstrated sacrifice through her long walks to her job in Houston, Texas, often walking on the hard pavement with a severed knee cap so she could help support our family.

Or my maternal grandmother who lived 250 miles away, who made sure her two grandchildren had nice shoes to wear to church.

To my mother (Clara M.), who pushed her children toward the goal of high academic achievement, while she worked double overtime to keep the utilities on in our house. Her tenacity and rugged individualism inspired me to strive to do better than my best.

To my father, who inspired my confidence and taught me to never settle for less as he always thought higher of me than I did myself.

To my paternal grandparents, who were always there to nurture my spiritual development as they vowed never to allow my sister and me to be separated from the church after our parents separated by divorce.

I owe a great deal of thanks to my patient wife, who has always encouraged me to pursue God's call upon my life.

I am also thankful for the prayer support, kindness, longsuffering; even financial support rendered to me by the Bethlehem Baptist Church family.

I thank God for Dr. Charles Wade, who served as Executive Director of the Baptist General Convention of Texas, and the people who serve our convention and allowed me the opportunity to inundate them with questions about the role of leaders in our more than 5,200 Baptist General Convention of Texas churches.

To the people of faith who poured themselves out to me by way of counsel, care, and even chastisement; Rev. Frank Lawson, C.D. Sammons, William (Bill) Lawson, Paul McBride, Howard Anderson, Leonard Hornsby, Roy Cotton, Gerald Davis, Uncle Richard and Mary Evans, James Culp, Michael Bell, Ron Cook, Charlie Singleton, Joe Ratliff, Crawford Kimble, A.E. Cleaver, H.K. Thomas, and many others whose lives inspired the body of this work.

The list of helpers and people who encouraged this work can be exhaustive, but there was one man God used to draw me near to the cross. His name was Charles Kevin Evans. Kevin was my uncle who was blessed with Downs Syndrome. He led me to Christ by demonstrating to me, and the people of the Philadelphia Baptist Church of Houston, the meaning of unconditional love; he was the embodiment of that love in every way. He knew every hymn the congregation sang; he remembered the prayers of the deacons and sermons of the pastor. He was the most beloved person in the church, and I wanted to be a part of that love. It was because Kevin wanted me around that I came to know Christ as my savior. Kevin was my Barnabas, and when I see him again in heaven, I will thank him for introducing me to Jesus Christ, who called me into a work that has shaped my life and now calls me to help shape the lives of the people I am called to serve.

Contents

CHAPTER ONE

Introduction

Whenever the news media reports on an incident in a Black neighborhood, or explains an issue that is relevant to racism along with other matters that affect the African-American community, or they want to provide an in-depth observation about the inner-city, often they turn to Black preachers. It is not surprising that many of the most well-known Black leaders in politics have the title "Reverend" in front of their name. Unfortunately, the same is no longer true among other ethnic group leaders. It has long been the criticism of many Black clergy persons that "We don't hear from our other ethnic clergy counterparts unless the matter is one of the hot-button moral issues of the day," and even then they don't speak for the community. While one cannot speak exclusively for any given group or community of pastors, many don't expect to hear from the clergy on matters that concern the community.

African-American clergy are expected to be upfront and outspoken on issues of Justice and Equality to say the least. The reason it is different in the Black community is because of the African-American church. The African-American church often referred to as the "Black Church," has a rich history of being one of the strongest institutions in the African-American community. Clergy and laity of the church have worked together for generations to make this possible. It was the church that was instrumental in helping a once oppressed people overcome slavery, fight racial discrimination, and endure economic hardship.

The nineteenth and twentieth centuries marked a time when the African-American church carved out a bold identity that is now in a state of flux. A changing African-American culture has morphed into a new community of people who are more affluent, better educated, and demanding new leadership models. In response to these changes, church leaders are challenged to move beyond the extensive use of the authoritative model of leadership to a more suitable participative inclusive style. If the church is going to remain relevant in our changing world, it requires a different approach and style of leadership.

This book was born out of a project designed to facilitate methods for helping African-American clergy and laity examine a variety of existing leadership styles. Many of these styles have not been formally explored or attempted in the church. My premise is that a thorough investigation into the usage of other existing leadership models will propel the Black Church into the twenty-first century.

One of the most basic leadership principles is that people will never advance beyond their leaders. Consequently, it is time for leaders of the Black Church to step forward and lead with a new appreciation for the changes taking place in the constituency. We're like Rehoboam, the son of king Solomon, who was not aware of the changing culture around him. Rather than listen to the wise counsel of his late father's advisors, he chose the path of stern authoritarian leadership. The result was the immediate split of the kingdom and the lost allegiance of ten of the twelve tribes of Israel (1 Kings 12). This book serves as a gentle warning to well-meaning church leaders who are only familiar with one mode of leadership. It is the hope of this author that the reader will take heed of the changing tide around him and make the necessary adjustments.

Along our journey, we will review the changing intra-cultural condition of the African-American church member, explore the possible implications of the changes on the church, and establish a biblical-theological foundation for the need of African-American clergy to re-examine their interpretation of the servant-leadership model taught by Jesus as expressed in the gospels.

This reexamination of leadership styles is crucial because the African-American church is suffering a drop in both congregational interest and attendance due to antiquated leadership styles, specifically the overuse of the authoritative leadership method. As simply as I know how let me say that if the leadership in the Black Church does not change the way it leads then the church is in trouble. We will experience the great "falling away" that is prophesied in the gospel (see Matthew 24:5-11).

A Brief Historical Overview

Beginning with the Post-Reconstruction Era of 1915 up to the Civil Rights struggles of the 1960's, especially in the southern regions of the United States, the pastor was one of the most dominant figures in the Black community. He (very seldom a female) was considered the person who was more in tune with the issues of the day (i.e. social justice, civic, state, and national affairs). He was, in most cases, one of the few people who were literate. Due to these advantages, he garnered a great deal of respect in the community. The pastor's words were held in high regard and carried a considerable amount of credence. An authoritative leadership style was most effective in this environment.

However, as time shifted, the disparity in the education level of church leaders and the church constituency began to fade. Individuals in the church, who were previously apt to follow the direction of the senior pastor based upon his insight and intellect, now sought to question the rationale of church procedures and programming. The overuse of the authoritative leadership model did not allow many willing participants to share their ideas of church growth and development with church leaders.

The result was a feeling of discouragement with the "old way" of doing things. Church members felt their opinion did not count. In many churches, the excessive use of this one leadership style proved devastating. Many congregations were marred by the single leadership approach and, to date, are experiencing rapid declines in attendance, participation, and growth. To add to the frustration among church members, many are now demanding their church leaders receive higher levels of training, adhere closer to their responsibilities as Shepherds, and return to the biblical model of servant-leadership.

Those church leaders and pastors who are not aware of the intra-cultural shifts among their congregants are stuck in a perceived bygone era of leadership. They are caught in a training vacuum or vortex that may lead to the decline of the African-American church as an institution. The loss of the Black Church as an institution would be devastating, and it would symbolize the total disintegration of the moral backbone of the African-American population. The entire social ethos and historical grounding of the African-American people would be lost.

THE IMPORTANCE OF THE CHURCH TO AFRICAN-AMERICAN PEOPLE

The church has served as the foundation from which the African-American culture was born. At the turn of the 21st century, the Pew Research Center reported that 87% of African-Americans say they are affiliated with a particular religious group, and 95% of those surveyed claim to be Christians.

"Although the role of professional clergy in the Protestant church at large was viewed as a vocation, African-Americans tended to treat their clergy as more than just employees of the church—they were royal tribal leaders for the community. So the separation between the sacred and the secular, the religious and the political, has not been as distinct among African-Americans. The clergy had to be advocates for justice, arbiters of internal disputes within the community and managers of sacramental affairs, all in one."[1]

A sizable percentage of Black clergy leaders have depended upon this rich heritage to continue, and it has allowed them to practice old leadership methods in a new century. It appears many have been lulled into a state of blindness regarding the changes in the mindset of the people they are called to serve. A strong sense of denial regarding the present situation of the more affluent, better educated and more socially acculturated

---

1   http://www.cnn.com/2010/OPINION/08/01/soaries.black.church/

African-American church member seems to have clouded once thoughtful and culturally sensitive minds.

People have changed because of a more tolerant and equitable system of laws and societal freedoms which did not exist during the early 1900's up to the mid 1960's; these are the vibrant years of the Black Church. People who were confined to the boundaries of their neighborhoods, unable to live in other sectors of the city, now reside in an altered world. Many are attracted to a congregation because it appeals to their new lifestyle made possible by their improved economic condition and educational achievement.

In many situations, church leaders have grown apathetic, and are not exploring the causes behind the decline in their attendance. It has led to a failure to seek an understanding of demographic shifts and the affect these frequent transitions have upon the psyche of the people. For the African-American church to thrive in a new century, the leaders of the church must become involved in the process of investigating the problem. The crucial issue is to determine how moving away from the traditional influences of the Black Church, both mentally and geographically, can provide opportunities for more diverse worship genres and ministry programs; it is a somewhat logical hypothesis for one who leads a declining congregation to consider. It is not lost by this author the reality that authoritarian leadership styles are not solely the governance model of choice for the senior pastor; many

African-American churches have suffered decline on behalf of stagnate thinking deacon and trustee boards.

Clergy must learn not to feel threatened by the increasingly more educated congregant who offers insight and input after exposure to more affluent congregations with multiple staff persons, planned education space, and organized committee structures. The pastor is called upon to accept the possibility that exposure to a broader culture invites an expansion of thought that can benefit the entire congregation. Such challenges to this mode of thought should not be viewed as a threat to anyone's authority, but rather as fuel, igniting an instinctive desire to learn more about the ever-evolving people he or she is called to serve.

Many people, especially those in positions of influence and power, feel threatened by change. Along with change comes the perceived risk of losing some of that influence and power that many before us have enjoyed. The operative term is "perceived." Only the person who is innately secure can allow others in the flock to "work out their soul salvation," under their leadership and guidance. Therefore, it is important to know that neither power nor influence is lost; it is gained. The way that those in power respond to change will determine if the change will be effective or not.

Consequently, before a transformation in the operational method of the church can occur, we must begin with a process of discovery concerning the new identity of the African-American church leader. We have examined various leadership models beyond the traditional author-itative model and discovered a great need for the Black Church leader to rediscover the role of a servant-leader as described in the New Testament.

A growing number of critics question the level of commitment African-American clergy have to making the necessary changes and shifts needed in order assure a successful ministry. Others tend to doubt if it is possible for many to adapt to new leadership styles. While many critics are oblivious to the history supporting the rise in prominence of the Black pastor, and the persecution of those who dared to "speak truth to power," the sentiment of the "Pampered Pastor" does exist. Negative images of Black pastors adorned in fine jewelry and endowed with big cars have hurt the church and jeopardized the survival of the entire institution. The problem is possibly one of perception and unfair stereotypical views of church lead-ers who are not in touch with the people. However, it can-not be denied that a growing number of people believe this image is the norm rather than the exception.

The life and legacy of the church depends on the pro-active efforts of its leader. An unwillingness to realize the positive impact a leadership image of humility and ser-vice can communicate may entrap the Black Church into a mode of decline from which it will not recover. While some clergy members may be satisfied leading a bare-ly surviving congregation, it can be argued that merely "surviving" rather than "thriving" is a precursor to death. To a growing cynical constituency, that approach might also jeopardize the promise for growth among younger potential church members. The only way for the African-American church of the twenty-first century to survive and thrive is for leaders to pursue a course of redefining their image and leadership styles.

Where Are We Now?

The African-American church community is in a period of transition. The community is no longer what it was a generation ago. Demographic studies and simple in-person observation show that the church constituency is also changing, becoming increasingly more affluent and educated. A great number of African-Americans are migrating from urban inner city areas into the suburban sectors of major metropolitan cities. Because of this change, a proliferation of people in this group who continue to be church members are demanding changes from the old authoritative style of leadership.

The changing culture and the more affluent class of African-American church members directly affect the modern church. Senior pastors are being challenged to explore diverse leadership models in order to lead this new type of congregation.

Proper execution of these models is crucial and has direct implications upon the future growth or decline of the membership. The Bethlehem Baptist Church, the church I serve as pastor, is a one hundred forty-seven-year-old congregation located in the Dallas-Fort Worth metropolitan area in the city of Mansfield, Texas. Geographically, the area surrounding the church was rural for more than one hundred and twenty-five years. The increase in the population of the city and the relocation of African-Americans from western and eastern states has caused a dramatic spike in growth at the church. Our congregation grew from seventy-five people in worship on an average Sunday morning in 1991 to more than five hundred in 2004, and now we worship with more than 1,000 on any given Sunday morning. Our social media reach takes us far beyond that number. In one generation, we went from being a small rural congregation to a large metropolitan congregation without changing locations.

The growth of the church brought a series of challenges, none more noticeable than the need for a significant change in methods of leadership. At the same time, my personal experiences as a church consultant with the Baptist General Convention of Texas combined with my experiences as a senior pastor for more than twenty-five years made it evident that a growing number of people preferred leadership styles which are inclusive and open to more input from the congregation at large.

When I first became the pastor at Bethlehem Baptist Church, I enjoyed significant power and influence over the decisions of the church. In fact, it was expected that the pastor was the one who "called the shots" and made the ultimate decisions. That is no longer true. Our congregation now consists of people who work in environments where they are in leadership positions, or at least in positions of influence. They are not eager to take off that freshly attained robe of power and influence when they come to church on Sunday, just because I'm the pastor. However, the influence I enjoy is based on my level of service to them and the opportunities for input that I provide.

In order for Bethlehem to thrive it was necessary for me to develop a new style of leadership; one that is conducive to a new, better informed, and more empowered congregation. I'm confident that sticking to the old authoritative style of leadership would have condemned Bethlehem to a declining rural-style congregation surrounded by a sprawling city. We would have owned one of the empty church buildings that can be found in every corner of the metropolitan area.

These changes in the church are what inspired the research for this book. I discovered that these changes are a direct correlation to the growth and decline of many Black Churches. The reader will discover that the research uncovered in this work is the relationship between the present attitudes expressed about church leaders of the African-American community and the current Black Church culture. Declining attendance and loss of interest in the church by a growing number of people was tied to very specific indicators. It is in the best interest of the African-American clergy community to understand, identify, and address the causes of growth and decline of the Black Church.

Research on pastoral leadership paradigms for the twenty-first century also revealed the affect demographic shifts had on the different mindset of African-Americans who served in churches located in rural, suburban, and urban areas.

Pastors and church leaders will benefit from findings which help answer questions regarding possible ideological shifts taking place in Black Churches. Research revealed some causes behind the level of apostasy, a leading topic of discussion during many conference sessions and meetings among Black pastors and lay leaders. The project gave attention to this real occurrence, which helps the African-American church confront what is likely leadership's failure to keep up with the changing times. Finally, my research on this topic provides help to arrest the destructive affects institutional ignorance can have on a once vibrant and thriving church.

During my research, I met with a representative group of African-American pastors and laity from various regions of the state of Texas in order to identify changes in the Black Church community. The purpose was to help church leaders find new models of leadership befitting the 21st-century African-American congregant. Interviews with pastors, laity, and potential church leaders, along with training conferences, questionnaires, and an evaluation instrument served as tools to help critique historic leadership models. An analysis of these models is necessary to allow for the development of options that will better serve us all moving forward.

The result of my research is contained in this book. The intent is to help African-American church leaders, and ultimately the Black Church community, to confront a present reality that a change and transition of thought are occurring among its constituency. Clergy leaders should be challenged to exhibit intentional efforts of servant-leadership by practicing leadership models that transforms their role from overlords to under-shepherds who humbly serve the children of God as willing slaves for Christ.

A biblical theological foundation, as well as primary and secondary results of the findings, will also be provided. We will examine the use of multiple leadership models that can be utilized by church leaders to preserve one of the cornerstones of the Black community, while also setting the foundation for future church leaders to build upon.

The authoritative style of leadership has served the Black Church well for a long time. However, our world has changed so significantly that such a style is no longer as welcomed or efficient as the sole leadership mode to ensure a growing, vibrant congregation.

I have lived in the Dallas/Fort Worth Metroplex for many years, and the area has changed enormously, especially in the past decade. The roads I traveled when I first arrived did a good job of getting me where I needed to be. However, with the changes and increased population, those old roads with narrow lanes with multiple stops no longer work efficiently. We have lived through an abundance of road and highway construction projects; sometimes the inconvenience has been extraordinary. However, once the construction is finished, everything works smoothly, and it is much easier to travel around the city.

We will discover together that creating some new roads of leadership will allow the Black Church to operate in a more biblical manner.

CHAPTER TWO

What Does the Bible Say About Servant-Leadership?

Then the mother of the sons of Zebedee came to Jesus with her sons, bowing down and making a request of Him. And He said to her, "What do you wish?" She said to Him, "Command that in Your kingdom these two sons of mine may sit one on Your right and one on Your left." But Jesus answered, "You do not know what you are asking. Are you able to drink the cup that I am about to drink?" They said to Him, "We are able." He said to them, "My cup you shall drink; but to sit on My right and on My left, this is not Mine to give, but it is for those for whom it has been prepared by My Father." And hearing this, the ten became indignant with the two brothers. But Jesus called them to Himself and said, "You know that the rulers of the Gentiles lord it over them, and their great men exercise authority over them. "It is not this way among you, but whoever wishes to become great among you shall be your servant, and whoever wishes to be first among you shall be your slave; just as the Son of Man did not come to be served, but to serve, and to give His life a ransom for many." Matthew 20:20-28 NASB

The phrase, "there's more than one way to skin a cat" has been around for a long time, perhaps as early as the middle of the 19th century. First appearances of the phrase also include the words, "so are there more ways than one of digging for money." Regardless of its origin, the meaning is clear. There are typically multiple ways to accomplish a task.

It is equally true that there is more than one way to lead a church. In my research, and in my experience, I have discovered a variety of leadership styles. Some are quite successful. Some work better in particular environments.

There is a lively debate among African-American scholars about the status of the Black Church today. Some take the position that the church is dead; having lost the voice that mobilizes the community, and even the nation. However, many others argue that the Black Church is still very much alive. My position is that the church is very much alive, but without significant change of leadership styles, staying alive is no guarantee.

Change of any kind is hard. Changing something that has worked for a long time is even more difficult. That is the reality faced by the Black Church. Making a change in leadership styles will be difficult, and probably cause many bumpy roads and detours along the way, but it is the only way the church will remain relevant.

The purpose of this book is to examine pastoral leadership models practiced by Black clergy and lay leaders. Listening to participants in numerous training events throughout Texas revealed that many people believe the time has come for African-American church leaders to explore the utilization of new leadership models rather than the old fashioned authoritarian model. This outdated model of leadership as the primary means of motivating people to do ministry has met with mediocre results and has led to hurt feelings.

Three key components highlight the perceived needs for clergy and lay leaders to motivate congregants to follow: (1) The pastor must develop a clear biblical understanding regarding his/her role as a Christ-like servant leader as instructed by Jesus in Matthew 20:20-28; (2) Church leaders must meet the new challenges of ministry by participating in on-going training opportunities as encouraged in 1 Timothy 4; and (3) The pastor must function in his/her call as shepherd-leader to guide people through a variety of leadership styles as presented in 1 Peter 5:2-4. The gospels reveal the disciples are more concerned about their potential positions of power and overall authority than an aspiration to serve people.

The scripture communicates a clear lesson regarding the problems and solutions facing the church. It also makes clear the goal for service that Christian leaders should aspire to attain. The passage quoted at the beginning of this chapter reveals the essential need for the modern church leader to rethink and change antiquated notions of leadership (see Matthew 20: 20-21).

The request made of Jesus regarding the desire of James and John for a special place in the kingdom exposes a haunting image of an often-used strategy played out in Black Churches all over America. Seeking internal promotions and influence, many are guilty of enacting similar tactics on display in this story. The scheme is one which has caused a significant number of potential leaders to abandon the church and accuse the institution of dynasty building.

Note the truths revealed in this story. James and John desired positions of power. The two men, who were part of the inner circle of Christ up to this point, were guilty of attempting to secure a place of prominence. While their mother is the person who makes the request in Matthew's gospel, it is important to note this section was an apparent revision of Mark's account.

James and John, the two sons of Zebedee, came up to Jesus, saying, "Teacher, we want You to do for us whatever we ask of You." And He said to them, "What do you want Me to do for you?" They said to Him, "Grant that we may sit, one on Your right and one on Your left, in Your glory." Mark 10:35-37 (NASB)

Matthew places the weight of the inquiry on the mother of the two disciples. She might have been Salome, sister to Mary, the mother of Jesus. To add insult to injury, not only can the indignant disciples blame Salome and her affection for her sons, but they can attribute her hope for their special treatment to kinship ties with Jesus. The lesson of service is frequently mentioned by Jesus. For example, He teaches on the subject in the synoptic gospels of Mark and Luke.

Sitting down, He called the twelve and said to them, "If anyone wants to be first, he shall be last of all and servant of all." Mark 9:35 (NASB)

...and said to them, "Whoever receives this child in My name receives Me, and whoever receives Me receives

Him who sent Me; for the one who is least among all of you, this is the one who is great." (Luke 9:48 NASB)

Even on this occasion, from a Jewish cultural perspective, the practice of one's mother asking special favors of the king, or others in authority was not new. For example, in 1 Kings 1:15-21, Bathsheba requests of King David that her son Solomon be made the heir to the throne of a unified Israel. Historians report the level of respect afforded to older women in comparison to younger women was well known in the Jewish culture. Jewish tradition provided aged women a special place of respect younger women did not hold (compare Judges 5:7; 2 Samuel 14:2; 20:16-22; Titus 2:4).

This tradition holds true today in the Black Church. The influence of the Church Mother, usually a long tenured senior/elderly female church member, has carried an equal amount of authority as many pastors, especially if the aged woman is the wife of a recently deceased tenured pastor. Her words were golden.

New Testament scholars have suggested the mother's request revealed the young age of the two men, implying she felt obligated to make the request on behalf of their best interest. While this theory is disputed, the fact remains the group did not fully understand the concept of leadership. In the context of the passage, Jesus attempted to teach a crucial lesson in light of his imminent crucifixion. Matthew points out the weight of the woman's request was clear; she (they) desired positions of power to wield authority, as seen in the mother's transparent appeal (see Matthew 20:21).

Use of the word "kingdom" may indicate a request asking the two sons be appointed or conferred power over their own jurisdictions. In other places, the term implies to install (1 Corinthians 6:4; Ephesians 1:20) or to sit to consider (Luke 14:28, 31). In essence, Salome was asking for her sons to be appointed to positions of authority. She was not only asking they be granted preferential seating in the new monarchy; she wants them to have a special place of influence that would suggest rule or lordship.

In response, Jesus called upon future church leaders to exhibit selfless service and sacrifice. Their motives were transparent, and the remaining ten disciples were not happy, or as Matthew 20:24 states, "(they)...were angry with the two brothers." Their anger was probably kindled because they possessed the same desire themselves, revealing the shared misunderstanding the entire group harbored regarding the meaning of service. It can be argued, the same measure of ignorance and utter disregard for selfless service still exists.

Church leaders are called to follow Christ as the ultimate example for servant-leadership. Jesus demonstrates in the Matthew 20 passage that requests for positions of honor or leadership is correlative of one's willingness to give of self in service to others. The type of service that pastors and lay leaders are called to offer simply invites us to operate in a self-giving capacity. The teachings of Jesus continue to be a lesson lost on many. Jesus presents an idea of service that is not the norm for the people of his time.

The social standards of the first century defined leadership to mean one who was designated as the greatest, and the position curried special favor that allowed the leader to be the one attended to by those who were subservient. The average citizen in Greco-Roman culture would see no difficulty in answering the question, "Who is greater, the one who serves or the one who is served?" The servant was almost always viewed as the lesser person. As the culture dictated the disciples' understanding regarding service and authority, so the African-American culture and the history of the Black Church has had a distorted understanding of the servant-leader approach to ministry.

One disingenuous practice of the times is the use of internal political pressure and family ties to curry favor. It is an age-old practice that has impeded the progress of the Black Church. In a similar approach, James and John attempted to use the influence of their mother to gain places of prominence in the eschatological kingdom alongside Jesus the Christ. Many attempt to use the political influence of others as a substitute for the divine call to service. Perhaps family and political ties work on some occasions, but they should not be used as leverage in Christian leadership.

One can clearly glean from the above passage that Christ was not at all impressed; neither are most congregations impressed with these familial connections. Leaders would be well advised to heed the lesson of service and sacrifice offered in Matthew's gospel. Jesus redefines the ultimate meaning of service by describing His own willingness to serve. He essentially said unless you are willing to serve like I serve then you are unworthy of a position of leadership. As we know from this side of the cross, His service was characterized by sacrifice, even sacrifice to the point of death. He directs his response, not to Salome but directly to the actual suppliants, James and John.

But Jesus answered, "You do not know what you are asking. Are you able to drink the cup that I am about to drink?" They said to him, "We are able." He said to them, "You will indeed drink my cup, but to sit at my right hand and at my left, this is not mine to grant, but it is for those for whom it has been prepared by my Father."

Jesus implies, with his response to the disciples, service requires more than what meets the eye when he asks, "Are you able to drink the cup that I am about to drink?"

New Testament scholar Donald Hagner gets to the essence of the concern of Jesus when he states in his commentary, "Jesus responds that the brothers (who are now addressed directly, as they are in Mark) did not know what they were asking. To be identified with Jesus' future glory means first to be identified with his suffering and death."

It was apparent the two brothers were oblivious to the fact Jesus was referring to their own impending persecution, and specifically for James, his martyrdom (see Acts 12:2). This is the case today. Few understand the cup of suffering which accompanies the minister of Christ on the journey. When confronted by the realities of serving God's people, the glory and the perceived glamor of the position are shattered when church leaders come to understand the stress and challenges that accompany the calling.

In the case of the disciples, the question "Are you able to drink of the cup that I drink and be baptized with the baptism that I am baptized with..." is not rhetorical, but real. The cup in the context of service is often used figuratively in texts of scripture relating to the issue of suffering, especially suffering God's wrath or judgment (Matthew 26:39; John 18:11; Psalms 11:6; 75:8; Isaiah 51:17, 22). The hard truth for church leaders is found in the need for them to understand they are being called to endure suffering.

In the 21st century context of congregational ministry, suffering can mean a number of things. For example: being called to endure certain hardships and high levels of emotional strain is, for many, a definition of suffering.

It may also mean the recipient of the hardship is called to endure attacks on their ego when he or she realizes they are not the center point of ministry. Suffering means absorbing humiliation when the flock refuses to offer you a pay-raise for the fourth consecutive year. The examples given are day to day experiences of hard-working men and women serving in vocational ministry. The aspiring church leader must confront the harsh truths of the Matthew 20 text which challenges them to be more than day laborers, but slaves.

The question posed by Jesus is fair. It should bring pause to all potential church leaders as if to ask "Do you think you...the individual, can handle the challenges that are before you?" "Can you drink this cup?"

These questions should be addressed to ministers at least on an annual basis. In the midst of ever-changing times, the following types of questions could also provide a place to start:

- "Do you think you can muster the patience to tolerate a more affluent people?"
- "Do you think you can face, with a spirit of humility, people who may be more educated than in times past?"
- "Can you, without pressure or prejudice, treat as colleagues those people who desire to express their true feelings about the mission, vision, and values of the church?"

- "Do you think you can answer the demands of to-day's congregant?"

JESUS HELPS ANSWER THE QUESTIONS

The next important lesson from the text is found in the fact that the church leader is called to unreserved service and sacrifice for the causes of Christ; without regard for their own well-being (see Matthew 20:25-26). To paraphrase, Jesus says, "You are not to conduct yourself after the manner of the leaders around you." Since the disciples were not accustomed to the form of uncompensated leadership being taught by Jesus, they expected to enjoy the rewards of leadership. The men fully expected a tangible benefit from their service in addition to places of position.

This is the case with African-American clergy and church leaders of today. A number of clergy in the African-American community have served as bi-vocational pastors for the majority of the years in ministry. It is the perception of some that African-American leaders serve anticipating material compensation and worldly prestige. It is not solely the fault of these leaders. It is mere human nature to desire some of the same pleasurable amenities that are enjoyed by members of one's congregation. Many people in leadership positions base their present leadership methodology upon what they've seen and thought was correct. Congregations in the past recognized the sacrifices made by their pastors and sought to compensate them or reward them for their labor. Scripture clearly states the importance of caring for the needs of the minister.

For the Scripture says, "You shall not muzzle an ox when it treads out the grain," and, "The laborer deserves his wages." 1 Timothy 5:18 (ESV)

Those who are taught the word of God should provide for their teachers, sharing all good things with them. Galatians 6:6 (NLT)

For the persons who do not understand the labor required to serve this new generation of parishioners it appears as if the pastor is being exalted, even garnering undeserved reverence. The point must be made that if such persons are allowed to participate more in the inner workings of the church and its missions and ministry, many of these stereotypical views will be debunked. In the past, the church has mainly taught future leaders to expect such treatment without offering full recognition of changing times.

The advantage of exploring a variety of methods is that it presents opportunities for church leaders to adopt new ways of leadership. The failure to learn new leadership methods is harmful to the life and health of the congregation. The struggle to encourage the exploration of ideas is similar in nature to what Jesus was confronting. The disciples were familiar with only one method of leadership, as is the case with many in the Black Church. The church is hurting because many leaders only know of one style of leadership. When that style loses effectiveness, the untrained leaders are unaware of different approaches. In addition, because of this blindness to different methods, they have failed to comprehend what is taking place around them.

Failure to develop new leadership models renders the leader out of touch with the people he or she is called to serve. The result of this conceptual gap has been frustration and may have caused once inspired leaders to abandon their posts in ministry when confronted by disappointment. Minister and author Lloyd C. Douglas states it best: "Ambition is attended by some grave dangers. Keep your ambition preserved in a solution of humility. Remember that the most eminent preacher who ever lived humbled himself and became of no reputation."

It is crucial to understand the meaning behind the term service. The degree of service, which is ultimately being communicated by Jesus, is made clear using two additional Greek terms *diakonos*, and *doúlos*. Gerhard Kittel, theologian and biblical language lexicographer, argues that both terms present a consistent clear message.

Christians are called to serve and not to be served. Jesus is communicating to his disciples, as well as to future followers, a message that says, "The greater one becomes, the more one is called to serve and give of their service to others." What is so utterly damning about the idea of serving as a slave in the eyes of the African-American culture is the picture that many descendants of former slaves have in their minds. The picture of people being packed away in the hull of ships like cargo to be sold on auction blocks like cattle, men used as breeders, and the many horrors individuals suffered provide an incredibly negative picture of a slave.

Western practices of slavery have skewed our understanding of slavery in the Greco-Roman world. The horrific manifestations of slavery as practiced in the American South make it difficult to understand the depths of devotion Jesus is calling his followers to emulate. A careful consideration of the command of Jesus will help church leaders explore various leadership models based on Matthew 20. Undoubtedly, a closer examination will reveal the historic facts regarding the responsibilities of a "Christ-Called Slave." For example, biblical scholar and author David Noel Freedman points out central features which distinguish first-century slavery from the form of slavery later practiced in the West during the 17th to the 19th centuries:

- Racial factors played no role; education was greatly encouraged (some slaves were better educated than their owners) and enhanced a slave's value.
- Many slaves carried out sensitive and highly responsible social functions.
- Slaves could own property (including other slaves!).

- Religious and cultural traditions were the same as those of the freeborn.
- No laws prohibited public assembly of slaves.
- Often, the majority of urban and domestic slaves could legitimately anticipate being emancipated by the age of 30.

A proper understanding of Christ's command to become a slave within the context of which Jesus was teaching, reveal that the slaves' individual honor, social status, and economic opportunities were entirely dependent on the status of their respective owners. For the servant of Christ, that knowledge stimulates encouragement rather than embarrassment. If one recognizes Christ as the Son of God endowed with all power, honor, and glory, is the master then that person, even as a slave in the Greco-Roman sense, is recognized as more honorable than most. The truth is that a proper understanding of the issue regarding one's status as great, or the ambition to be great while serving God, will reveal it is not a travesty, sinister desire, or bad thing to serve God in pursuit of greatness. In fact, according to Jesus, serving God is the only way to receive greatness.

Christian leaders must be fully informed about what it means to be great. This information will lead to an examination of their motivation for doing ministry. Motivation for ministry does matter. For the potential leader or individual who is called to serve Christ, that motivation is a process of discovery. The process includes an ongoing internal and external dialogue driven by curiosity into the meaning of ministry.

For more than a century the African-American pastor has enjoyed an enormous amount of freedom regarding his or her place of authority. The enticement of power and prestige has made the transition to shared ministry and service difficult for some. As Keener stated in his article on the Matthew 20 passage, "Absolute power always corrupts precisely because the desire for power over others, to whatever extent one may achieve it, shows that people remain slaves to (another's) self-centeredness."

The pastor who is serving in this new era of ministry is called to heed the words of Christ, which could be paraphrased, "We do not exercise dominion over our people." Jesus makes the point that as one aspires to be great, even with the temptation of power and absolute authority, he or she must be a servant. Jesus further emphasizes the point when he says, "...but whoever wishes to become great among you shall be your servant, and whoever wishes to be first among you shall be your slave" (Matthew 27:20).

The African-American church leader who moves past the limited understanding of pastoral authority actually demonstrates a good understanding of Jesus' teaching. Jesus is calling upon His disciples in the Black Church to view themselves as servants in the best sense of the word. The Christian idea of service represents a "...trans valuation of values, especially in the African-American church tradition."

A stark reality in the African-American community is the long-held understanding the leader or the pastor is the shepherd; not in the sense of First Peter chapter 5 (discussed later), but according to a misunderstanding of the term "shepherd." This improper designation is provided in the words of Jesus in Matthew 20:25, "...rulers of the Gentiles lord it over them."

As unpopular and arrogant as that attitude may sound, history bears witness that the pastor is the leader of the people. He has been held in high esteem. Drunkards have hidden their bottles in the presence of the pastor. He has been the one person who has held sole authority in the church body and the surrounding community.

The point is, the shepherd has reigned supreme, and it has been the belief that he was put in charge by God. Many have used Jeremiah 3:15 (KJV) as justification for their authority: "And I will give you pastors according to mine heart, which shall feed you with knowledge and understanding."

Others have justified the role of the shepherd by the text in Hebrew 13:17 (KJV) as proof of authority: "Obey them that have the rule over you, and submit yourselves: for they watch for your souls, as they that must give account, that they may do it with joy, and not with grief: for that is unprofitable for you."

The bold suggestion to engage in dialogue leading to the development of a new pastoral leadership paradigm from an African-American perspective goes against conventional wisdom. Yet, the time for redefining the mode of leadership is upon us. Many portions of the Bible teach Christians to strive for excellence in the service of the Body of Christ. Paul wrote to the Corinthians, "But eagerly desire the greater gifts." (1 Corinthians 12:31, NIV). To Timothy, he wrote: "Here is a trustworthy saying: if anyone sets his heart on being an overseer, he desires a noble task" (1 Timothy 3:1, NIV). Again, he said: "So, whoever cleanses himself [from what is ignoble and unclean] who separates himself from contact with contaminating and corrupting influences will [then himself] be a vessel set apart and useful for honorable and noble purpose. Consecrated and profitable to the Master, fit and ready for any good work" (2 Timothy 2:21, 34, NIV)

Therefore, it is of utmost importance to provide spiritual service with consummate excellence and then leave the success of service to the Lord. Jesus, in Matthew 20, is teaching his disciples a new way to serve. This new reality is that true servanthood does not garner a great deal of recognition. After one grasps the concept, the next phase in the transition is putting into practice a means for acquiring the self-discipline needed to serve consistently as *doúlos* (slave). Jesus drives home the point by saying, "but whoever wishes to become great among you shall be your servant, and whoever wishes to be first among you shall be your slave." A firm grasp of this lesson will help church leaders progress to the next critical developmental stage of discovering new leadership paradigms, which is training.

Chapter 3

Leadership in the Black Church

The historical situation of Black Churches being clergy-dominated stands in need of change. If not, the church will not continue attracting gifted persons into the membership. This will mean utilizing the many talents of church members in all aspects of church life, especially leadership roles. The result will be better trained and more involved laity in the mission of the church. To stay the course and do nothing will lead to tragic consequences for the church.

The problem is exacerbated because the culture and character of the African-American church has changed.

Gone are the days of the typical southern style worship of the Black Church. Worship is still heart-felt and emotionally expressive, but is done with the aid of contemporary technology and music styles. African-Americans have more choices and a variety of demands on their time. Sunday morning church attendance now competes with youth sports activities, shopping at the mall, Sunday morning golf, and an array of other activities. The days are gone when the church located in the heart of the community was the only place people could encounter genuine friendship, freedom, and positive reinforcement in a "not so friendly" world. Many larger Black Churches are now located in suburban areas, surrounded by people who live a typical suburban lifestyle.

The social movements of the 1960 played an enormous role in shaping the contemporary Black Church. In addition, the rise of megachurches impacts not only these new large congregations, but also the small congregations that continue to exist. There are several important factors to take into consideration:

- A means to combine black consciousness and Christian ethics
- A role for the rapidly expanding black middle class and its relocation
- A more professional and highly literate laity demanding higher quality

- Changing gender roles and how it effects women in ministry.

Along with the change in the culture came a change in the mind-set of the people. African-Americans began to take advantage of educational opportunities, and the desegregation of the market place has led to more affluence. People no longer need to depend on the lone voice of the pastor. Individuals who could only find their voice or chance for upward mobility in the church can now compete for positions of leadership and authority in the secular society. The shift has caused people to view the church and its leaders from a different vantage point.

The "powerful all-knowing pastor" is now seen as a colleague, someone to work with, not a person to take orders from. Simultaneously, the reality that individuals other than church leadership possess ideas about the direction of the church has become a point of contention around church conference room tables. The problem is that many clergy leaders failed to understand and adjust to the change. Scores of pastors complain about the decline in church membership and the decrease in weekly offerings. Many are puzzled and express befuddlement in pastor's conferences and seminars. They fail to understand why things are changing.

The African-American laity provide a sobering perspective. Many blame church leaders for their failure to connect with this new group of people who populate their churches. Their critique is that leadership styles have failed to "keep up with the times." The perception is that the level of leadership training in the African-American church has failed to keep pace with the growing affluence of its constituents. Congregants migrating from the urban centers to the growing suburban communities are demanding better quality leadership and programs.

It has been suggested that a problem many Black Churches experience is the opinion that the pastor is considered to have a greater moral stature than he truly possess (see Romans 3:23). This view has given the pastor a great deal of autonomy. Consequently, in some cases the pastor has been credited a level of reverence and devotion that approaches idolatry.

The truth is that he must help the congregation know that he has human frailties that are similar to their own. While he must be afforded the respect needed to lead, he cannot be deified. If the church is centered on a single personality, other than Jesus Christ, the entire future of the church hinges upon the abilities of that person to maintain a certain level of super humanness that is impossible.

Moreover, such worldly adoration is unhealthy because it allows the laity to dodge their responsibilities of service. The result of such misplaced adoration stunts the growth of the church because it allows all of the weight of missions and ministry be placed on the shoulders of a single person. Therefore, the successes, and most often the failures, of the ministry are placed on the pastor. He is called to serve. The idea of making anyone other than Christ the focal point of local church will doom the church to failure.

Yet, it is no secret church constituents are demanding an increased quality of service in the areas of homiletics, discipleship training, children and youth ministry programs, and the multitude of other ministries offered by the church. Many church lay leaders seek a pastor who can do everything but walk on water, and in many cases demand that he serves as a bi-vocational pastor; even scoffing at the idea that he should expect fringe benefits. It is often an unfair balance of demands placed on the pastor of a church. The change that is being proposed not only needs to take place at the level of the clergy, but also in the minds of the black constituency.

To satisfy the demands of this new church makeup, the change must start with the leadership. Leaders must find their way through change by revisiting the pathway to service and servanthood as set forth through the word of God. It is common in the hierarchical composition of many traditional African-American churches with an autocratic structure or chief executive officer format not to allow other voices or opinions be heard. Therefore, the need for change and transition must have its origin with the traditional power base—that is, the pastor. It is also imperative that this change be biblically based.

A biblical foundation for the feasibility of such a paradigm shift can be found in the gospels, discussed in the previous chapter. Jesus' teaching in Matthew 20, along with supplemental writings from 1 Timothy 4, followed by and concluding with a passage from 1 Peter 5:2-4, support the theological basis for a new leadership paradigm in the Black Church. Several lessons can be learned from the Matthew passage which relate directly to the need for developing new pastoral leadership models for the twenty first century. Leaders are challenged by the words of Jesus to abandon old models for gaining positions of authority. It is necessary to understand the magnitude and the responsibilities that accompany leadership positions, and redefine what is meant by authority, service and sacrifice.

Jesus explicitly states in Matthew 20:25 that we are not to "lord over" each other; instead we are to serve one another. It is important to mention that this does not give license to disorder or chaos, but it does imply that clergy leaders must exhibit a life that makes it clear that God's people are to be treated with dignity and mutual respect. The true servant leader earns the respect that is given to him/her by the congregation. The twenty-first century does not afford the clergy leaders the blanket visa of authoritative leadership as in the past. Today, more than ever, one must demonstrate the gifts of servanthood in the spirit of 1 Timothy 4:14.

Do not neglect the gift you have, which was given you by prophecy when the council of elders laid their hands on you. 1 Timothy 4:14 (ESV)

While the clergy-person is not mandated to "lord over," he is obligated to give "oversight." As the person offering oversight, there is a natural spiritual recognition that the pastor is not the "owner" of the flock, he is the "keeper" of the flock. The flock belongs to God, we are serving at His pleasure.

Shepherd the flock of God that is among you, exercising oversight, not under compulsion, but willingly, as God would have you; not for shameful gain, but eagerly; not domineering over those in your charge, but being examples to the flock. And when the chief Shepherd appears, you will receive the unfading crown of glory. 1 Peter 5:2–4 (ESV)

HISTORICAL ROLE OF THE AFRICAN-AMERICAN PASTOR

The African-American culture and the Jim Crow South created a position of authority and an impenetrable institution to be matched only by the industrial engines of the Northern sector of the United States. Historically, the primary role model and person of prominence in the African-American community was, for more than one hundred years, the pastor. He was the person looked upon by the community as the advocate for the rights of the people in his congregation.

It was widely known that the Black pastor, after the abolition of slavery, was one of the few literate people in the community. Due to his value in the sight of the people as the chief spokesperson and spiritual guide of the community, people were encouraged to attend to the basic welfare of the pastor and his family. The pastor was the most respected and well cared for individual in the Black community for more than a century after slavery and well into the 20th century. His position was one coveted by other males in the community who considered themselves articulate and well read. Segregation and lack of education among former slaves made the church the only place one could be respected as an individual.

The Black Church was the place where hospitals and schools were born and flourished until the late 1960's. While integration and gentrification are co-equal reasons for the decline in the need for such initiatives it is also important to note that the unwillingness by many church leaders to invite ideas from a more economically savvy constituency in the view of many, has hurt the Black Church. The unintended consequence is the further deterioration of transformational influence among an increasingly more potential church member. The most direct path to closing this gap between church leaders and church members is through intentional efforts of

retraining church officials to refocus on the biblical principles of leadership and service.

AFRICAN-AMERICAN CHURCH LEADERS IN THE 21ST CENTURY

African-American church leaders facing a changing
landscape in the 21st century should not run from the
challenge or reject the changing perspectives of their
congregants. Instead, they must rally to the familiar
truth expressed in the old Baptist Covenant prominently
hung on the front walls of many older African-American
churches that states, "We engage by the aid of the Holy
Spirit to walk together in Christian love."

The helping hand of Christ is the only means by which
aggravated church leaders can redirect their congregations toward a vibrant recovery. Several pastors have said
they are too old to change, resigned to serving the people
God sends them, and will simply allow younger pastors
to worry about the challenges of the day. Herein is the
challenge for new leadership models.

One might think, with the declining numbers of people attending churches which refuse to allow flexibility in
their leadership modalities, the exploration of new methods of leadership would be welcomed. However, that
is not always the case. It may be that the frustration so
many church leaders encounter while serving local congregations is found in their reliance on outdated leadership methods. Christian leaders need to learn that their

success depends on their willingness to learn new things and receive training and counsel from others.

The notion of "me against the world" is what prohibits clergy from reaching out to others and taking advantage of continuing education opportunities. An often-misunderstood defense mechanism is clergy leaders who feel the need to demonstrate they are more knowledgeable on most subjects than others. The result of this tendency is to overcompensate in those areas in which the person is less knowledgeable and leads to mismanagement, improper counseling practices, and other inefficiencies. In some cases, the individual convinces himself that he knows more than he really does.

This attitude makes it quite difficult for church leaders to surrender their positions of power because the feeling of infallibility can become intoxicating. This feeling of power and invincibility can cause the evaporation of the idea of self-sacrifice and service which were the original intent of that person's calling. If this is not reality, it is the perception of disgruntled former church members in the African-American church who believe their leaders view themselves as superstars rather than servants. It is the "superstar" characterization that entices many to further distort who they are actually called to be—servants and not lords.

If the African-American church is to change in order to remain relevant to the changing African-American community, then that change must begin with the leadership.

Black Church leaders who are unwilling to share their leadership responsibilities and temper the perceptions of power and prestige that are exacerbated by some of the trappings of their position will make it impossible for the church to remain a positive influence in Black communities. Unfortunately, most disgruntled church members have no idea of the woes of leadership, and what they often see as glitz and opulence is only a cover for the pains that accompany the responsibilities of ministry. The old adage that no organization rises above its leadership is universally true. It is equally true that no leadership can rise above its self-development. In other words, we must not wait for someone to do it for us. Current church leaders must step up, learn the necessary tools and methods to inspire transformational leadership, and provide the kind of leadership today's church needs in order to remain relevant.

Adjustment is required of both pastors and local congregations. The expanding roles available to clergy are changing everything. At the same time there are many clergy who feel threatened by these new challenges. It is important for them to learn that their faithfulness will be rewarded and they will continue to thrive as they share the decision-marking process with a wider circle in the church community.

Chapter 4

The Pastor as a Servant Leader

Numerous terms could be used to describe Jesus. Among those would be "servant" and "leader." He was a leader who did not hesitate to take off his robe in order to wash the feet of his followers. He was a servant who demonstrated leadership in the way he stood up for those who had been wronged, like the woman caught in adultery. Jesus provides the definitive example for church leaders to follow.

Sadly, this type of leadership has not been as widely advertised as the model most highlighted or practiced in the African-American church. While scores of

African-American pastors are hard working bi-vocational servants, many people stereotypically view the Black Pastor as a "strong arm" leader who merely barks out orders. However, those who serve as clergy in the church are well aware of the sweat and tears that accompany such a difficult and often thankless divine assignment. Traditionally, the Black Church has granted a significant amount of autonomy to those who occupy its pulpits. Consequently, the pastor has been ascribed a level of reverence and devotion that for some has been characterized as "idolatry" on the part of those who make up his local church congregation, and for no other reason than that he is the pastor.

While this is an unfair categorization by those standing on the outside looking in. It is no question that such worldly adoration is unhealthy because it feeds into the ego of the stereotypical view of the African-American clergyman as pastor, not to mention those whom he is called to serve, by making a mere man, not Christ, the focal point of why that local church exists and, conversely, why those who attend that church should continue to do so. Thus feeding the frenzy and offering the unbeliever even more reasons for not attending or participating in the activities of the church. This kind of behavior is leading to the decay of the institution.

These stereotypical views of the African-American church must be debunked, and it begins with the pastor. Many of these stereotypical assumptions regarding the

Black pastor cause other leadership groups in the church to challenge the authority of the pastor which upsets the traditional balance of power. The result is a rudderless organizational structure that is inept and unable to function. The challenge is to offer a leadership strategy led by the pastor that allows for participation from others while maintaining a clear organizational structure.

A great deal of credit must be given to the new generation of church leaders who are vowing against attempts to gain power and position thwarting pastoral leadership. Such power struggles are becoming less popular in the Black Church due to the changing demographics. The place of the pastor in the heart of the African-American church continues to rank high. The goal is to include the ideas of other stakeholders who can advance the vision of the body. A well-intentioned servant-leader will be intentional about pointing the church toward Christ and instilling a renewed interest in Jesus' words recorded in Matthew 20; these changes offer hope for a healthier future. In order for this dream to be realized, some specifics need to occur.

CHURCH LEADERS MUST PARTICIPATE IN ONGOING TRAINING OPPORTUNITIES

Today's clergy must meet this challenge by taking part in continuing education opportunities and resisting the temptation to pursue absolute power within the congregation. Often, clergy assume enormous levels of responsibility without accountability. To assure real change takes place in the Black Church, a process of re-training must be sought.

The apostle Paul highlights the importance found in the need for clergy and church leaders to examine their present practices of leadership. He sheds additional light on the process in the Pastoral Epistles. It is argued that the character and conduct of leaders was the primary concern Paul was addressing in chapters two and three of First Timothy. In response to the actions and activities of the leaders in the church at Ephesus, character is more important to Paul than duties.

However, it is important to note the lack of discipline and training among the leaders was apparently the catalyst behind the apostasy taking place in the church at Ephesus. The spreading of false doctrines had to be stopped. Timothy possessed the gifts necessary to perform this ministry. The Apostle Paul's role was to encourage Timothy to do the task and train the new leaders. In 1 Timothy 4:6-16, Paul urges Timothy to "...put these instructions before the brothers and sisters..." and fight the good fight.

We can draw similar conclusions regarding the Black Church. If present practices of pursuing one-sided leadership models continue, the result will be a declining church with misguided leaders.

In pointing out these things to the brethren, you will be a good servant of Christ Jesus, constantly nourished on the words of the faith and of the sound doctrine which you have been following. But have nothing to do with worldly fables fit only for old women. On the other hand, discipline yourself for the purpose of godliness; for bodily discipline is only of little profit, but godliness is profitable for all things, since it holds promise for the present life and also for the life to come. It is a trustworthy statement deserving full acceptance. For it is for this we labor and strive, because we have fixed our hope on the living God, who is the Savior of all men, especially of believers, and teach these things. Let no one look down on your youthfulness, but rather in speech, conduct, love, faith and purity, show yourself an example of those who believe. Until I come, give attention to the public reading of Scripture, to exhortation and teaching. Do not neglect the spiritual gift within you, which was bestowed on you through prophetic utterance with the laying on of hands by the presbytery. Take pains with these things; be absorbed in them, so that your progress will be evident to all. Pay close attention to yourself and to your teaching; persevere in these things, for as you do this you will ensure salvation both for yourself and for those who hear you. 1 Timothy 4:6-16 (NASB)

Just as Timothy was encouraged to train or discipline himself to maintain a godly lifestyle, it is important for modern day leaders to heed the same advice. Paul recognized that, while his son in the ministry was involved in the practice of exercising self-discipline, he was, in turn, encouraged to share proper instruction with those people who were not teaching correctly at the Ephesian church. Paul advised Timothy to administer his instruction to the Ephesian Christians and redirect the spiritual and doctrinal movement of the church while he was undergoing spiritual development himself. Paul's role as mentor, along with his words of encouragement and instruction, are an example of the role senior leaders in the African-American church community should play.

The place of senior leaders in the Black Church tradition cannot be overstated. The elder statesmen who are the senior tenured pastors in the life of the African-American church hold a position of great authority and high esteem. Many pastors will admit they have adopted the mannerisms and even the leadership styles of their spiritual father in the ministry. Like Paul, the elder pastor's influence in the life of the younger minister is an essential component in their personal growth and development process.

It is important to mention, people such as Dr. Gardner Taylor, the late Dr. E.K. Bailey, Dr. Charles Boothe, as well as Texas legends Dr. William (Bill) Lawson and Dr. Marvin Griffin, have made the matter of academic and spiritual preparation primary during their lectures and sermons for several years. However, the slow decline of many traditionally led African-American churches has sparked a great cause for alarm and spurred a sense of urgency.

Paul's relationship with Timothy is an example of the role influential church leaders within the confines of the Black Church community should have. Declining attendance in the African-American church ought to encourage present leaders to say to our future pastors, administrators, associate ministers, and others, "train yourself!"

The apostle uses the term *gymnázō*, which in the literal sense means to exercise naked. Timothy is encouraged to do ministry void of the temptations which surrounded him. Not unlike the African-American church, the misinformation propagated by members of the Ephesian church was affecting the entire congregation, and most notably the leadership. The erroneous doctrines of the false teachers were dangerous. Paul makes the point that the goal for Timothy was to correct these actions. That could only be done if the young church leader prepared himself for the task ahead. As the leader, he was called to correct these false doctrines and then lead in the proper direction.

The lesson for the modern-day leader is found in understanding that a minister cannot lead effectively without receiving proper training. What does this mean for the aspiring African-American church leader who is held in high esteem? A closer look at the need for training will reveal two striking similarities of note between Timothy and many African-American pastors.

First, it is necessary to understand that the minister's status in the eyes of the people in the community has an effect on the church. Second, Timothy was to be aware of his role to become a model minister to others. The reference to both points are highlighted in 1 Timothy 4:12, "Let no one look down on your youthfulness, but rather in speech, conduct, love, faith and purity, show yourself an example of those who believe."

The church leader as servant of Christ is challenged to uphold a standard of excellence despite his or her age. At the same time, the person is called to be a good example to others. Both points are necessary for successful ministry. The characteristics regarding speech, conduct, love, faith, and purity were distinct qualities lacking among other so-called leaders in the church at Ephesus.

Timothy was also to recognize he was going to be viewed by the community as a role model. Thus, he was encouraged to live his life in accordance with that knowledge. As stated by Towner and Marshall, Paul attempts to communicate to Timothy that he is to act in such a way as to be an example of godly living, with the implication this will win him the respect of the other people who may be measuring him by human standards.

Church leaders like Timothy are encouraged to learn that by living an exemplary life, his behavior becomes an

active force of transformation for the entire community. The apostle Paul states in 1 Timothy 4:13-16, "...until I
come, give attention to the public reading of Scripture, to
exhortation and teaching. Do not neglect the spiritual gift
within you... Pay close attention to yourself and to your
teaching."

In conclusion, the work required is the act of stripping
off the influences of one's environment. Shawchuck and
Heuser refer to such initial work as the need to attend to
the interior attitudes of the leader. The message is clear
to leaders: attending to oneself requires lots of self-anal-
ysis. Heuser referenced the great church reformer Mar-
tin Luther who taught that the last activity of each day
should be to examine one's motives and actions.

The introspective leader is one who becomes sensitive to himself and the sensitivities of others. In the context of the African-American church, leaders are being
challenged to strip away old ideas of authoritative leadership models. Potential leaders are being encouraged to
strip away ideas of grandeur which hinder so many. The
actual act of stripping away of thoughts and outdated
practices leads to the exercise of self-examination. The
practice of self-examination will cause leaders to question the actions of senior leaders from their past, whose
practices may have impacted the church negatively.

One can hope pastors and laity alike will begin to take
advantage of the growing number of workshops and seminars becoming more available. It is this type of attention

to the obvious need for training which may help bridge the gaps forming between traditional church leaders and their congregations.

THE PASTOR CALLED AS SHEPHERD LEADER TO LEAD THE PEOPLE

The apostle Peter gives an urgent exhortation regarding the need for African-American church leaders to explore different leadership models.

...shepherd the flock of God among you, exercising oversight not under compulsion, but voluntarily, according to the will of God; and not for sordid gain, but with eagerness; nor yet as lording it over those allotted to your charge, but proving to be examples to the flock. And when the Chief Shepherd appears, you will receive the unfading crown of glory. 1 Peter 5:2-4 (NASB)

Peter's refrain to pastors calls them into account regarding the need to give their all to secure a brighter future for the church. As stated above, the church leader living in the 21st century who seeks continued training in his or her attempt to serve God's people better must be aware of their real motivations for doing ministry. Shawchuck and Heuser alluded to this in their work by inferring, "the influence of your walk, character, and integrity is the most powerful motivation you have on the congregation's attitude and performance." Thus, the pastor as leader is to understand his or her call requires more than the average nine to five job or career work day.

Ministry actually becomes the person. Donald E. Messer takes the point further by referring to the fallacy of the idea of vocational ministry serving as a mere career move as a modern heresy. Ministry is not a career; it is a way of life. One does not work as a minister; one becomes a minister. The apostle Peter makes it clear for the reader to understand the gravity of his responsibility.

Leaders are reminded they are the *presbyteros*, the elder or shepherd. The Holy Spirit has appointed them to be overseers (bishops) and shepherds over the congregation. Peter's pronouncement to them as shepherds is significant. The weight of the future of the church was on the shoulders of these leaders since the apostle made known to them the whole counsel of God. They had to administer the legacy of the apostles and follow the examples passed down to them by Jesus.

The shepherd or elder was charged with protecting the church against the danger of false teachings and harmful practices that threaten the congregation from without and from within.

The responsibility has not changed to this day. It is imperative for the African-American pastor to understand the gravity of his position. In addition, it is imperative to understand the impact their leadership has on upcoming generations of leaders. Most importantly, he or she is called to execute these duties as outlined by Peter.

In the sense of this text, the pastor is charged with the functions of oversight, guardianship, and guidance. Much like the shepherd imagery borrowed from the Old Testament depiction of God leading the Hebrew slaves through the wilderness during their exodus from Egypt, so must the 21st-century leader proceed. The challenges may be different, but the pastor, as shepherd, is responsible for the well-being of the sheep.

While serving the sheep is an important responsibility, the shepherd must also understand his or her authority is limited. Peter teaches in his writing the one lesson church leaders—ordained or otherwise—must learn is that the "flock" is not the property or sole possession of church leadership. The "flock" is under the ultimate ownership of God.

Leaders in the Black Church have mistakenly attempted to claim members of their church as their people. Others have gone as far as labeling the congregants in their churches as "My Negroes." The usage of these titles and descriptions has given way to a false sense of entitlement, causing many clergy leaders to believe they can treat church members as less than common people. This false sense of ownership allows many in leadership positions to become desensitized to the needs or the growth and development of the people entrusted to their care.

All of this means the leader, as servant, is to exercise the responsibilities of a shepherd in the spirit of humility. Failure to understand the people of God are to be treated as the flock of God makes it difficult for leaders to render themselves humble. It also causes church leaders to overlook their responsibilities as stewards of God's possessions.

The authors of the text, *Shepherd Leadership: Wisdom for Leaders from Psalms 23*, suggest modern day leaders should understand the role of the shepherd in antiquity. Gaining a clear picture of the primary duties of the shepherd will clarify distorted views of the role of church officials and people in authority. According to the authors, shepherding was a business, in most cases; a twenty-four-hour occupation that involved protecting and feeding a flock owned by another individual. The shepherd was responsible for the complete oversight of the flock.

Per co-author David Davenport, the leader does not become the shepherd until this concept is understood. He or she must grasp the truth that any action taken or decisions made on behalf of the flock can either improve or damage the quality of life of the flock forever.

This truth certainly applies to the Black pastor who withholds opportunities of advancement from his or her respective congregations. Failure to expose God's people to new ideas and modes of service can be characterized as starving the flock. Unfortunately, scores of people leave the church because they can no longer remain a member at a church that is "going nowhere in missions and ministry."

The act of shepherding connotes spiritual feeding which will nurture the people of God and inspire them to action. One can argue that the church has suffered due to the stifling of ideas and failure of the designated authority figures to participate in the act of feeding of the flock. A marred view of one's call as "Elder" is possibly the reason why many congregations are unable to reach their set goals and God-granted potentials. Peter offers these words of wisdom to help the church leader or group of elders to remain focused on the tasks of their calling.

Another important lesson taught in Peter's epistle is the emphasis on the attitude of the leader. The 21st-century leader should note the change in our times. For more than one hundred years, people of color were not afforded the freedom to move ahead in venues other than worship, entertainment, academic scholarship, hospitals, and the like. The institutions of racism and segregation made the Black Church one of the few places for African-Americans to find an outlet from day to day labor. As a result, leaders developed a certain air of arrogance because the church was the place that met most of the needs of the people. The leaders of the church were well aware they were the center of the Black community and to be disconnected from the church was to be further separated from society.

As times have changed and conditions in society have improved, parishioners now have choices for worship, entertainment, education, and other activities. Church leaders who hold to antiquated ideas built on the congregant's need to associate with their church—and their church alone—are living in a bygone era. Others who are victims of their own overblown perception of their place of authority are also living in a state of fantasy.

Peter makes it clear one is not to lead under compulsion. The compulsion to which he refers is clearly a vice and not a virtue. For example, one should not lead due to pressure or lead with a reluctant spirit. Today's leaders must adopt an attitude which communicates to all people they are serving willingly and cheerfully according to the will of God. This person understands "many are called, but few are chosen."

Peter's writing further emphasizes the need for the motivations of leaders to be pure. He mentions a negative motivation which must be avoided: serving for the purpose of sordid gain or, as stated in the King James Version, filthy lucre. Peter expressed obvious concern some may attempt to enter into the gospel ministry for the purpose of personal enrichment. The very notion of ministers serving churches to enrich themselves has further eroded the once positive perceptions of leaders.

The goal of the 21st-century leader is to debunk these false ideas. Peter reveals he is not an advocate of any individual who prostitutes the name of Christ for the purposes of idolatrous prosperity. The Christian leader of the 21st century is encouraged to understand economic motivations for ministry can be a detriment to effectiveness in service and can hurt the potential for gaining the trust of the people he or she is called to serve.

The terms filthy lucre or sordid gain can apply to other areas of self-indulgence beside the category of personal enrichment. *Aischrokerdōs,* or eagerness for base gain, also means to participate in a vocation for the purpose of greed which satisfies itself through fraud. The African-American church has stood as a symbol of God's power at work through a once oppressed people. The stability of the church has symbolized the stability of a people whose faith has sustained them through many of the transitions of American history. The leaders of the church have served the people with an enormous amount of courage, integrity, and honor. However, the need for a new type of leader has emerged. When leaders are confronted by the sentiments of disillusioned congregants, it is hopeful a change in overall leadership practices will ensue.

Peter's letter to the church links the readers to the teachings of Jesus. To paraphrase Jesus as he taught Peter and the other disciples in Matthew 20, "You know that the rulers of the Gentiles lord it over them, and their great men exercise authority over them... it is not this way among you..." Peter encourages the leader of the church to be eager and demonstrate a sense of zeal which will bring glory to God and God alone. This is a person who displays a ready mind, one who understands that he or she is serving at the pleasure and for the purpose of God's good will.

The text implies one is not only to love what he or she is called to do for the cause of Christ, but that person is warned against the temptation of serving for the sake of gaining power. He or she is cautioned against the practice of lording it over those whom God has placed under his or her care; instead, the person is to serve to the point of self-sacrifice.

In conclusion, the leadership of the African-American church must become serious about what appears to be the decline of their tradition, and take all measures to save and reinvigorate their congregations. The pursuit of new leadership models will cause those who are entrusted with the responsibilities of congregational oversight to be reacquainted with a biblical understanding of service. The notions of serving people for the benefit of the people serving will be challenged.

A re-examination of the term *doúlos*/slave will transform the stigma of the word from the historical blight caused by American history to the Greco-Roman usage of the term. An investigation of new paradigms for leadership will help to adequately inform subsequent generations of the essence of their calling as individuals who will entrust their entire well-being into the care of Jesus Christ as the ultimate guide of their lives.

The need to grasp a biblical theological hermeneutic for servant-leadership will lead many to understand the privilege associated with the call to ministry. The innate urge to serve God's people will be another indicator that Jesus Christ placed a desire within his chosen vessels to lead people to salvation. The urgency of the moment is not unlike that of Timothy in Ephesus. The environment is rife with a diversity of doctrines which lure unsuspecting disillusioned church members into their ranks, making the need for proper training urgent.

The challenge is great, but the goal of reclaiming the lost has not reached the level of hopelessness. The degree of sacrifice proposed to leaders is in the form of "sharing the reins of service" so others may receive spiritual benefits of discipleship. The foundation for building stronger churches is set; this project is calling leaders to be reminded of a more radical view of service and sacrifice which requires continued training and ultimately *lýtron* (the forfeiture of one's life).

Chapter 5

What are People Thinking?

If you have paid attention to the news the past couple of years, you have noticed an increased emphasis on polls. It seems like there are polls on nearly everything —who are people going to vote for, how do people feel about something, what do people consider the best option. The list of questions and polls is endless. It is a reminder of the importance we should place on the opinions of individuals involved.

The genesis of this book was a doctoral project I submitted concerning pastoral leadership models in the African-American church. A significant element of that project included interaction with Black Clergy and Church Lay Leaders. These conversations and listening sessions provided much of the insight for this book. It was a detailed undertaking in order to understand the current thinking of clergy and lay members of Black Church community. This information is important because if we expect people to make significant changes, we must first understand what they currently think and know.

As we have already noted, the Black Church has experienced cultural and ideological shifts which have created a demand to examine current leadership practices. I considered leadership models for the 21st-century African-American church. The project highlighted the differences that exist in leadership model preferences between rural and urban churches as well as the relevance for authoritative leadership models in the 21st century. The significance of the role of laity in the African-American church regarding their place as both leaders and partners was scrutinized. In addition, the cultural and ideological shifts which may affect the mindset of the African-American congregant were studied. The following information is a compilation of the findings from the research.

The discovery process involved information gathering and listening activities with Associate Ministers and laity which helped provided direction. Laypersons sensitive to leadership issues were enlisted along with Associate Ministers who had not served as senior pastors. The group was charged to consider six specific leadership models and styles critically. The models include, (a) Authoritarian, (b) Consultative, (c) Participative, (d) Visionary, (e) Supportive and (f) Hands-Off (Laissez-faire).

The next step included interview sessions, questionnaires, and material for pastors and laity. Each participant was asked to identify their style or mode of leadership and identify a model of leadership from their past. Participants were asked to explain their rationale for utilizing one form of leadership over another. After the process of the identification of a particular style or combination of leadership methods, participants were asked to evaluate their style and how they might choose to lead in the future.

The third step required group participation with a mixture of laity and pastors. This included the sharing of preliminary research findings, which involved an historic explanation concerning the "Rise of the African-American Preacher" and the rationale behind his historical status in the Black Church. Respondents also received an overview of the research findings on the demographic shifts among the African-American community. The participants offered insight on the possible implications of the research data for their present ministry assignment.

The fourth step involved two evaluation sessions; both sessions were scheduled for two hours in duration. The group evaluated the demographic findings, possible intra-cultural implications on the African-American church, and offered their feedback and suggestions for use of the results of the research.

Five meetings were held in addition to the interviews and additional research conducted to examine pastoral leadership models. The five sessions included church leaders and laity from a variety of locations. Each meeting was designed to include church leaders and laity from rural, urban, and suburban churches, as well as churches with small to mega size memberships.

The findings and results that emerged for the project are presented in this chapter. At the outset, let me reiterate that the findings confirm what we have been saying from the beginning about the need for change in the Black Church.

The literature review revealed there is much history and support for the authoritarian leadership model of the African-American church, and that history still influences church leadership today. It further revealed there are many historical perspectives for leadership in the church, and more specifically, the African-American church. Many leadership models were found. However, for this project, the six designated models of leadership offered in John J. Westermann's *The Leadership Continuum* are most pertinent for the 21st-century African-American church.

Westermann provided the following models for consideration: authoritarian, consultative, participative, visionary, supportive, and hands-off (laissez-faire). The definitions of the methods are as follows:

- Authoritarian – The leader who makes decisions with little or no input from participants. The primary style is to direct workers to carry out the task as given by the leader's direct command.

- Consultative – The leader listens to the group members to learn their perspective; the leader is willing to change his/her decisions based on a convincing presentation of useful ideas from those he/she leads.

- Participative – The mode of leadership which allows both involvement in decision-making and some autonomy in tasks for workers. The leader delegates to others some responsibility and authority to make decisions after explaining the problem and outlining the boundaries from which to operate.

- Visionary – The leadership method which allows workers to generate alternative solutions, decide, and identify the problem. The role of the leader is to identify the particular issue requiring a solution. The group will determine the means necessary to solve the given problem.

- Supportive – The role of the leader is to help the group achieve whatever it decides is the priority for the organization. The leader serves as the coach, understanding the group is virtually autonomous to decide the core of the problem at hand

and the solutions needed to obtain the optimum outcome.

- Hands-Off (Laissez-faire) – The style of leadership that does not require the leadership's participation at any point of the problem-solving process. The leader's presence is virtually non-existent.

This information was utilized in the focus groups to lead discussions. After a brief overview of each model, discussion ensued regarding everyone's early experiences in the African-American church. The following is a presentation of the findings from this research.

THE EFFECT OF A RURAL PERSPECTIVE

The first finding was the discovery of a rural perspective regarding leadership modalities versus an urban perspective of leadership. The initial respondents were primarily from rural areas where they are accustomed to meeting for worship on designated Sundays of a given month (i.e. 1st and 3rd Sundays). This group described how the clergy leadership depended heavily on the participative model of leadership.

The participative model relies heavily on the commitment of the laity to be involved both in the decision-making process and carrying out the necessary responsibilities to complete the assigned tasks. This form of leadership required some autonomy in tasks for workers from the pastor or primary lay leader in the congregation.

The key congregational leaders' job was to delegate to others a certain degree of responsibility and authority to make decisions. In addition, functions were designated only after boundaries were set from which to operate. The discussion period and questionnaires showed this form of leadership was the norm, not the exception.

Many of the conference attendees reported the participative trend of leadership offers individual parishioners more opportunity to engage in the process of church leadership. Per African-American church historian E. Franklin Frazier in his work, *The Negro Church in America*, most church leaders of the time operated from the authoritarian modality. However, our study showed this was not the case in rural churches. Frazier appeared to rely mostly on urban or inner city churches. The use of the participative model was proven to be more widely used in rural settings.

The above finding is a polar opposite of what was the case in the formation of the African-American church in the southern region of the United States after the period of slavery. Due to the composition of the church being organized in the manner of a family structure, the dominant male retained the responsibility of providing sole direction for the congregation, outlining its mission and mode for survival. Thus, the pastor's words were held in high regard and carried a considerable amount of credence. However, the discussions revealed a shift that took place when it was realized the rural church could not support a full-time pastor. In the context of the discussion, one participant highlighted the rationale for a high dependency on the laity. It was expressed as follows, "...there was a need to depend upon the laity and lay leaders to foster the survival of the church."

The result has been an evolution of leadership styles, and it became evident and prudent for those African-American churches located in rural areas to adopt such models (i.e. participative, supportive, and the like). Even more profound, the participative and supportive models were also found in the urban church settings. The demographic shifts which took place may have also contributed to the retention of the participative mindset among the new African-American urban populace. Therefore, research reveals the rural practices of African-American churchgoers were more influential than realized by conventional wisdom.

The surprising amount of participative leadership we found in churches has been caused by the need for survival. Churches in rural areas as well as urban churches faced with a dramatic demographic shift have both learned how to spread the responsibilities of leadership to a wider circle. This is the lesson that must be learned by the African-American church as a whole if it is going to continue to enjoy a place of prominence and influence. This situation seems to prove the old adage, "Necessity is the mother of invention."

RECONSIDERING THE AUTHORITATIVE MODEL

A second significant finding was the consensus from participants in the belief that absolute authoritative leadership stifles growth. This was the sentiment of many, especially the younger pastors who participated in the process. One pastor even noted, "...that the days for sole authoritative rule or 'Lordship' were over."

Another participant commented, "Authoritative leadership can backfire and negatively affect the impact churches can have on accomplishing the great commission given to the church by Christ." Taking the sentiment further, one could also sense the pastors and laity were expressing an adverse reaction to this form of leadership because its continued use or abuse may be a direct violation of the belief of what it means to be Baptist.

An example of the adverse effects of the sole use of the authoritative leadership motif is its failure to encourage ownership of the charged task from the people assigned to the activity. Often, it was noted that a major problem with this method is the lack of commitment demonstrated on the part of the individual carrying out the order. The tendency for the person receiving the assignment is to execute the request without possessing the motivation needed to produce a high-quality outcome. It was also suggested that failure to involve individuals in the planning process could obligate them to projects for which they had no passion, thus causing the desired effect of the ministry task to backfire.

Church growth strategists discourage the exhaustive use of the authoritarian leadership modality. When pressed upon individuals, the authoritative model not only leads to less passion toward the ministerial effort and project, it erodes the sense of fellowship in the church. The result of the over usage caused irreparable damage in many African-American churches and led to a constant decline of the entire Black Church as a whole.

This is a good paraphrase from conference participants: "If the person is simply obeying an order, the success or failure of the effort lies with the person who issued the directive."

They could not have been more adamant in their attempt to convince fellow clergy and laity in attendance that using one mode of leadership was not good for one's ministry. It is evident if one does not demonstrate a long-term sense of commitment, the real effect of the project will be short-lived, affecting the ministry and missional impact of the church in future endeavors.

It is important to mention involvement for the people at the conference meant to involve others in the planning or decision-making process; understanding the spiritual development of the person could be stifled. For example, one student minister explained she does not frequently practice the authoritative leadership modality because she wants, even needs, her students to own the ministry.

She stated, "To own something you need to do more than just hear what 'I' the 'Director' thinks; you want to know what the student thinks from their level of understanding."

The implication made by respondents is that the repeated use of authoritative leadership is a violation of the governing practices of a Baptist church. If the pastor believes in the basic tenets of the Baptist church, he or she cannot overlook the binding principles that support a shared belief among most traditional Baptists. Young pastors and laity expressed an understanding that many African-American church members now recognize God calls and gifts given to every believer for service in His kingdom.

Thomas S. Rainer and Daniel L. Akin in their work, *Vibrant Church: Becoming a Healthy Church in the 21st Century*, called this principle of participation by involving the congregation in the decision-making process "congregationalism." Hence, the criticism from the majority of people participating in the focus sessions was the unstated belief the abusive use of the authoritarian leadership model is anti-Baptist, and not consistent with a foundational understanding of how Baptist congregants identify as a "saved people" in the sight of Christ.

It is also correct to add, casting theological objections aside, it is a poor practice to put all authority in the hands of one person and expect extra-ordinary results. While all things must be done decent and in order and the congregation must agree together to follow the leadership of the pastor; the fact that the church is a voluntary institution means members have the freedom to participate or not. However, those members who choose not to participate in the process not only abdicate their responsibilities to help lead the church toward the goal of saving souls, they also miss the chance to allow God to work through them by the exercising of their innate gifts and talents. Widespread participation is enhanced when more and more people are included in the decision-making process and those persons share a willingness to support the agreed upon vision and direction of the congregation.

At one time, the average southern African-American congregant would not have thought about their personhood in the church in comparison with their identity outside the church. In other words, they felt the same about themselves in both environments. That has changed. For example, it was a given fact that a blatant inequality existed in the daily life of most African-Americans during the period of the Civil Rights struggles. Therefore, no comparison was made between the treatment of a person in church compared to the way that person was treated in the workaday world. The church was the place where even the most oppressed could find their personhood. It was the harbinger of equality for an oppressed people.

The church was the one place where one's status was lifted, especially if the person was a preacher, deacon, missionary (female preacher), or church officer. The negative sentiment expressed by the participants was a reaction to a deeper feeling of resistance to any kind of arresting motive which would deprive people of their freedom. Articulated, it would mean a violation of one's understanding about being a part of the priesthood of believers, as interpreted as explained by Peter.

But you are a chosen race, a royal priesthood, a holy nation, a people for God's own possession, so that you may proclaim the excellencies of Him who has called you out of darkness into His marvelous light; for you once were not a people, but now you are the people of God; you had not received mercy, but now you have received mercy. 1 Peter 2:9-10 (NASB)

Even more offensive, it's seen as a violation of the identity of individual believers in relation to God and the church. It was stated by one participant, and affirmed by others that, "The church consists of individuals who have committed their lives to God through the expression of their faith in Jesus His Son." The impression given from the views of most in attendance at the focus groups was that it is inconsistent to fail to involve people and the giftedness endowed upon them by the saving power of God through Christ Jesus, our Lord.

Ultimately, the repeated infringement upon the rite of creativity could also violate the understanding of another highly esteemed doctrinal principle of "soul competen-cy." It is understood that every human being possesses the skill to interpret and apply scripture or determine matters of faith and practice for oneself. Resentment was expressed by a respondent in reaction to practices he deemed as unnecessary and futile. The result is ministry which does not matter and people who ultimately do not care.

IMPORTANCE OF THE ROLE OF THE LAITY

A third major finding was discovered when eighty per-cent of one group of pastors agreed the role of the laity was important in keeping their churches alive. To inter-pret the nuances communicated, it appears as if the fear among most was the harm which could be afflicted on the Black Church if leaders fail to recognize the adverse effects of uninformed leaders for generations to come. One female clergy person viewed the authoritative lead-ership model as a method which did not allow others to express or exercise their own God-given gifts and talents. Noted African-American church historian C. Eric Lincoln warned against the inability of clergy to recognize a shift in the mindset of the congregation as being detrimental to future church growth.

Churches and pastors who are not aware of the val-ues shift in their congregants are stuck in a perceived by-gone era of leadership and training, which may lead to the decline of the church as an institution. Failing to utilize

the gifts and talents of more educated and affluent people will stifle the growth of the African-American church.
The repeated use of those leadership models which fail to
grant opportunities for colleagues will render the church
unattractive. Unbelieving middle and upper-middle-class
African-Americans who now enjoy relative freedom and
equality outside the church will tend to find the church
restrictive.

These sentiments were echoed numerous times by
pastors who espoused the most passionate concerns
about upholding the authoritarian model as the mode of
leadership in which they were most comfortable. After
reviewing the dialogue and questionnaires from older
pastors, it was evident each group recognized the need
to receive consensus from the laity before the execution
of ministry tasks in order for their church to both survive
and thrive.

LACK OF AWARENESS OF LEADERSHIP MODELS

The last primary finding was discovered at the culmi-
nation of the focus groups. A large percentage of the individual participants indicated they were not aware that
other named leadership styles existed. While other models were described, such as participative, consultative,
supportive, and visionary, the pastors and laity were not
able to attach names to the leadership methods.

After familiarizing each group with Westermann's six
named leadership models and forming an understanding

of leading from the continuum perspective as opposed to static step by step usage, most agreed leadership involved a combination of models and not one style in particular. In respect to a small number of participants, some were aware of the importance of leading from more than one mode. Some expressed they were presently leading by a continuum because it allows for better utilization of individual talent.

This lack of knowledge of other leadership styles reinforces the notion that additional training is required in order for the Black Church to be able to utilize each member to their greatest potential. Understanding the process will lead to more widespread participation.

Secondary Findings

The above findings are secondary and were viewed as more helpful to the African-American church community, but there were some pleasant surprises brought forth during seminar discussions and focus group dialogue.

The Need for Continuing Education for Clergy and Laity

The first secondary finding was the need for clergy to begin the process of attaining additional education. It was discovered that both clergy and lay leaders uncovered deficiencies in the areas of theology, evangelism, counseling, youth and children's ministry, family ministry, and other Christian education themes. As previously mentioned, the challenges for many churches are well known and documented; the leader is called to muster the courage to prepare for a phenomenon occurring in real time. Each of the respondents in all the focus groups acknowledged the need for church leaders to learn more and train as often as possible on those matters directly connected to their ministerial settings.

On the same topic of professional development for clergy, C. Eric Lincoln (Professor of Religion and Culture, Duke University) writes: "The evangelical traditions of the past which set the norm for the emergent black denominations only required evidence of a sincere call from God to the ministry." A prudent policy for the future would add professional education and a full-time clergy to that norm. The natural fractures of life in the Black community will increasingly require full-time attention from professionals fully prepared to give counsel, leadership, and support in an era in which the traditional reservoir of humanitarian concern is increasingly depleted.

A DIVERSITY OF LEADERSHIP PRACTICES

Another secondary finding disclosed that practical knowledge of the named leadership styles was being utilized in the African-American church community in a variety of forms. It was enlightening to disprove the researcher's initial hypothesis that "most Black Churches were governed by authoritarian leaders." On the contrary, church leaders realized the importance of involving people in the decision-making and planning process to assure the survival of the church.

One pastor mentioned his past experience while serving under the guidance of his father, which involved the visionary approach to leadership. He revealed to the group of participants his belief that the church of his childhood had changed, and continued to thrive to this day because the pastor was willing to share his vision with the church. Even more of a surprise to him was that a designated name existed for a style of leadership he experienced dating as far back as the late nineteen sixties and early nineteen seventies.

It is important to mention that the visionary form of leadership, as well as the others described in the research, has biblical foundations. Regarding the visionary approach as defined earlier, one can recall the leadership of Jesus on the occasion of his ascension to the right hand of the Father. In Mark 16:15-20, Jesus outlines for the disciples their mission, the goals for their mission, and the outcome of their work based upon their obedience to follow what was set before them. The result is seen in the number of people who claim Christianity as their religion and the countless number of prospects yet to profess Christ as their Savior and Lord.

THE BLENDING OF LEADERSHIP STYLES

The blending of leadership styles is another secondary finding. While engaged in interviews, pastors, a Baptist Student Ministry director, and lay leaders described the blending of leadership styles, such as a combination of participative and consultative, or participative and supportive. The participative form of leadership continues to surface as a favorite because it appears this leadership method communicates a spirit of partnership. In the Apostle Paul's first letter to the church at Corinth, he writes to them in the third chapter about foundational principles for living. He attempts to make the case for partnership and unity. After chiding the church on their divisive behavior and their practice of separating into various parties (i.e. Jesus, Cephas, Apollos, and Paul), he says they are not rivals at all; instead they are "fellow laborers." The idea is that we are all "partners" in ministry together with Christ.

For we are laborers together with God: ye are God's husbandry, ye are God's building. According to the grace of God which is given unto me, as a wise master-builder, I have laid the foundation, and another buildeth thereon. But let every man take heed how he buildeth thereupon. 1 Cor. 3:9-10

People who share a common interest will be passionate about what they do; in our case, it's ministry. Jim Collins, the author of, *Good to Great: Why Some Companies Make the Leap and Others Don't*, repeatedly says that those people who retain ownership of an idea are more committed, and they need less motivation. The fact that they feel ownership of the vision and are partners in the accomplishment of the task at hand is enough to drive them forward daily.

SUMMARY OF FINDINGS

In conclusion, each session we conducted ended with extraordinary consensus regarding the use of a variety of leadership models as a common practice. It was also agreed that leading along a fluid interchange of leadership models would better serve their congregations. Based on the information acquired from the group participants, leaders using a diversity of styles tended to grow while those who did not struggled and even declined.

The challenge seems to be daunting, yet one hundred and forty-two years after slavery, the African-American church is faced with a new reality. The new reality which cannot be denied by this project is that African-Americans are finally becoming less African and more American; in our religious ideology, politics, behavior, and social practices. The Black Church leader can meet these challenges with confidence if he or she is willing to develop a pastoral leadership model for the twenty-first century. Leaders will inevitably be challenged to explore the needs of the people and discover those needs are in constant flux. The reality for leaders is to understand if there is a resistance to change, he or she might be found without a church.

Chapter 6

Cultural Considerations

The Bajau people are refugees who are not allowed on their native land in the Philippines, so they have built a life by living in the ocean. As incredible as it sounds, they have built wooden huts that literally rise above the sea water. They spend their days fishing on boats and platforms. They are able to take their boats to the nearby land where they trade their fish for rice, drinkable water, and other necessities.

This is an almost unbelievable example of how people can adapt to a change in the environment. This chapter is about change. Nothing as significant as changing from living on land to living on the water, but rather a change in culture. A cultural shift almost always disrupts the status quo and necessitates an alteration of the organization. This is what is happening in the African-American culture.

Several important factors play a significant role in the shift in mindset of the African-American church constituency. These cultural considerations have proven to be primary influences in the way churches respond to a changing people. Key factors of interest include an increase in education, rise in affluence, and demographic and geographical shifts.

EDUCATIONAL ADVANCEMENTS

Research has shown the level of educational attainment among African-Americans has increased significantly over the past fifty years. Since the 1940's, African-American educational levels have continued to climb

- In that year, just 12.3 percent of Blacks ages 25 to 29 graduated from high school.
- By 1965, more than half of African-Americans ages 25 to 29 graduated from high school. Today, per the Census Bureau, 86.2% are high school graduates.
- In 1997, the percentage of African-American youths graduating from high school almost paralleled white young people—86% of Blacks ages

25 to 29 were high school graduates, compared to 87.6% of Whites

This change has pastors and lay leaders making adjustments to their leadership styles, and those who have not yet gotten the message need to start paying attention. In the book, *High Impact African-American Churches: Leadership Concepts from Some of Today's Most Effective Churches*, George Barna and Harry R. Jackson agree the leader sets the tone for the upward mobility of a more affluent church constituency.

Researchers have revealed African-American congregants are more likely to seek fulfillment of service through the utilization of their own skills and abilities. The task of the church leadership is to give clear direction of the mission, values, and ultimate goals of the church. The church that is clear about its path will feed the imagination of congregants. There will also be a spirit of ingenuity shared by this emerging group of people.

The changing culture also must reconsider the current suspicion regarding the leadership role of women in the church. The growing number of women pursuing seminary degrees has increased to a level where many are demanding to assume the titles of their male counterparts. In the past, women were the leaders in many churches but did not require the use of titles, such as Reverend, Minister, or Deacon. For more than one hundred years, many female authority figures in the church settled for titles like Church Mother, Deaconess, Missionary (Female Preacher), Evangelist, Stewardess, Sunday School Teacher, and Vacation Bible School Director. That has changed, and it is evident that the changes in our society are the reason. The educational advancements of African-American women are well documented and cannot be ignored.

- There was a 219% increase in the percentage of black women taking their first professional degrees.
- The percentage of blacks who received doctorates in education and theology was nearly that of whites; it also observed that law and medicine have attracted a higher proportion of blacks than any other race.

The challenge for male church leaders is to reconcile the importance of their own call from God with their role as God's instruments for making disciples of Christ. Once they realize they are not to reproduce clones of themselves, they will be more willing to extend the ministry to women.

INCREASE IN AFFLUENCE

In addition to the educational achievements of African-Americans, another factor which has led to the shift in culture is the rise in affluence among the

African-American community. The significant improvement in the economic plight of African-Americans has affected the mindset and living habits of many. The increasing wealth of many African-Americans has brought greater demands upon the quality of programming they are being asked to offer. However, the increases in income among the congregants has, for many, not yet transferred to the treasury of the churches. Giving in many of the churches represented in the focus groups has remained static, despite growth in income as shown in demographic data.

- According to the 2000 U.S. Census data, the increase of affluent African-American residents in the Dallas/Fort Worth area rose at the remarkable rate of 205% overall from 1990 to 2000.
- A study by The Brookings Institution of Washington, DC, showed the movement of Blacks from urban areas to the suburbs is very high, especially in areas like North Texas and Atlanta, Georgia. Dr. John Logan, a professor of sociology at Brown University, remarked the demographic shift of African-Americans is like that of Anglos who migrated from metropolitan areas in the 1950's and 60's.

The shift from urban to suburban neighborhoods reveals a marked increase in income above the national average of $41,994.00 to well over $100,000.00 per household. The increased income or affluence creates other demands, which may prove challenging for traditional leadership models. Yet, the pastors and laity who participated in the study group were puzzled why the constituents who were demanding more programming or enhanced quality in church programming did not understand their vital role in contributing financially to the cause.

Paul L. Wachtel says a change wrought in one's mind regarding his or her own self-identity can ultimately change the entire society; however, if the change is without understanding of its effects on the society, it can lead to disaster. Wachtel's comments speak to this disparity between the desires of this more affluent group and the dollars needed to fund these demands. One must conclude, once again, it is the task of the leadership to take up the mantle of training to inform the congregation on the importance of stewardship and contribution to the growth of the church. It is important to mention that "growth" does not only imply an increase in numbers, but an increase in volunteer participation, evangelism, and children and youth ministries, just to mention a few.

As people are moving to the suburbs, a definite shift is happening in Black Churches. For example, Blacks and Hispanics are contributing a greater share to the growth of suburban and exurban counties in large metro areas. The *USA Today* article made clear that 53% of all

African-Americans live in the Southern Sector of the U.S. and the number is growing. Thirty-nine percent of all African-Americans now live in U.S. suburban areas. They desire better homes, better jobs and schools, tend to be middle class, and are college educated.

Our discussion groups revealed the cultural shift brought with it mixed results. Respondents located in the more rural areas mentioned the migration of people to the suburban areas near large city centers has hurt them. Leaders argue many of the people who remain behind tend to acquiesce to the status quo and are less likely to be motivated to participate in ministry activities. The challenge for the leader is not to lose his/her sense of purpose. It is well noted the leader sets the tone by demonstrating the passion and the drive needed to encourage positive results in ministry despite the environment. When clear strategies are set with clear objectives, the possibility for success grows.

Conversely, those living in high growth areas expressed a different set of challenges. The challenge of these individuals was expressed through both excitement and anxiety. Excitement was the dominant emotional expression as the church leaders talked about the potential growth of their congregations, specifically numerical growth. Anxiety was expressed when the same respondents began to assess their present ministerial structure, both leadership structure and programmatic.

Most of the people anticipating growth had not yet started to prepare for it. The leadership in many of the churches located in the high growth areas had also not studied the cultural mindset of the people. Most admitted that their staff or volunteers had not participated in any training to enhance or start new ministry activities, which would meet the needs of this new, more progressive people. Again, the key finding regarding the admitted lack of preparation was the obligation of these churches to prepare for growth or allow the growth curve to overwhelm their churches.

Finally, the most important and most noted factor affecting the change in the cultural mindset of African-American church members has been their view of authority figures. Not confined only to the Black Church, but the transgressions of high profile individuals of the faith have brought a sense of mistrust of authority. In every area of life, we need assurance that our leaders act with integrity. This applies especially to the Christian world. Our ministers must be people of integrity. The work of church leaders is built on truth, not just trust in their ability, but confidence in their spiritual and ethical wholeness.

When a nationally known preacher is accused of mishandling finances in a way that has enriched him personally, or a well-known pastor in our own local community get caught up in an immorality scandal, it has an effect on your church. It is particularly the case today with our over-abundance of communication; no church exists in a vacuum. People bring their experiences with them when they gather on Sunday morning.

It is well documented that a positive attitude toward clergy and others in church leadership has waned over the years. In many case, this has occurred when individuals were placed on a pedestal too unbalanced and too lofty to maintain. While a great number of clergy who are in touch with their humanity fully understand they cannot "walk on water," it does not dim the glaring spotlight which shines upon them. The concluding thought on this finding comes from noted Jewish ethicist Rabbi Abraham Joshua Heschel. When asked his thoughts on the actions and lifestyle of young people in the late 60's and early 70's, he replied: "Let them remember that there is a meaning beyond absurdity. Let them be sure that every little deed counts, that every word has power and that we can, everyone, do our share to redeem the world, in spite of all absurdities and all frustrations and all disappointments. And above all, remember that the meaning of life is to build a life as if it were a work of art."

There is no doubt, as the African-American culture changes and people attach to competing systems of belief, the challenge for church leadership is to answer the call of Christ to seek and save those who are lost. Demographics change and culture is always in flux, but the one unalterable truth is that the church has been called to proclaiming the saving message of Jesus Christ—a message that does not change.

It is unlikely that your church is being forced to relocate and live in the ocean. However, it is quite probable that you are experiencing significant cultural change that can be equally devastating if you are not equipped to adjust to the change. Church leaders must take the necessary measures to prepare themselves to be able to lead the congregation that God has entrusted you to lead.

Chapter 7

Reflections

When I began an examination of the leadership models in the Black Church, I started with the hypothesis that most African-American church leaders were leading from an authoritative leadership model. That had been my experience growing up in church and something I had tried to eliminate in my own ministry approach. I was troubled because leading from the authoritative model on an exclusive basis is inconsistent with the servant leadership model taught by Jesus to the disciples. Jesus' teaching recorded in Matthew 20:20-28 serves as the primary scriptural passage for the theological premise of the model of leadership to be enacted in the 21st century. It teaches a potential leader that his or her role is to be a servant of all people without any expectations for compensation or accolades.

I had also assumed that the historic role of the African-American pastor made the task of converting to the servant leadership model a difficult feat to attain. This difficulty is caused by more than one hundred years of prominence for the Black pastor and traditional African-American church leader.

However, after an extensive research project (see Appendix for details), I encountered a mixture of challenges to my original hypothesis regarding the role of clergy in the church. Every individual who was interviewed, surveyed, or tested during the focus group sessions, regardless of gender or tenure in the church, believed they understood the Matthew 20:20-28 definition of servanthood.

The notion that servants of Christ were to be servants of all people was not a foreign concept in the minds of the participants. Matthew 20:25-27, which implies the church leader is called to unreserved service and sacrifice for the causes of Christ without regard for their own well-being, was accepted as a point of fact. The lessons regarding the disciples as *diakonos* and *doúlos* were clear. It was understood that service is meant to be selfless. That lesson was made clear in the focus group sessions. *Doúlos*, as explained in the Greco-Roman context of slavery, involved the total surrender of one's personhood for the well-being of others. In the United States, the infamous version of slavery mars the Greco-Roman imagery and has caused ire or disdain; but not so in the minds of the focus group participants.

Perhaps most surprising in the research was to hear participants offer excuses to defy the teachings of Jesus on the matter. For example, one pastor suggested that ministerial circumstances, such as the level of maturity of his congregation, were the reason he used the authoritative model as his primary method of leadership. Another mentioned a lack of trust in the ability of the congregation to make decisions without the input of the pastor as his reason for utilizing the authoritative model. In another instance, it was simply clear defiance against the notion the pastor should not be the one person in charge of all church matters as the reason for his leadership methods.

These responses strengthened the motivation for my research and proved that clergy must connect their theological and biblical beliefs to their actual practices when conducting ministry. The implications of rejecting what is made clear in Matthew 20:25 is the temptation to overlook other ethical issues. The matter of service and the radical notion of rendering oneself as a slave cannot be taken lightly. The individuals who voiced these sentiments were serving churches that had plateaued or were in decline. In fact, since that time, two of the congregations have all but dissolved.

It is evident that some church leaders have been spoiled by the high esteem placed upon them by past generations of once oppressed, less affluent people.

Jesus' teaching on servant leadership brought to light the difficulty of breaking away from the practices of the dominant culture of which one was called to serve. The average citizen in Greco-Roman culture would see no difficulty in answering the question, 'Who is greater, the one who serves or the one who is served,' because the servant was almost always viewed as the lesser person. They had a hard time seeing the world from Jesus' perspective.

In a similar fashion, participants in our study also found it difficult to face the reality of the changing times. While they fully demonstrated a clear hermeneutic of their role as leaders in light of the gospel teaching, from a practical perspective, they struggled with confronting the realities they face in their actual field of ministry.

One of the most encouraging discoveries was the willingness of the participants to make changes. That is a significant step because any type of change is difficult, but a change in behavior is especially hard. Church leaders are quite open to the concept of servant leadership. The struggle is with how to implement the idea without destroying the influence of the past.

However, as I have already noted, the rapidly changing mindset and makeup of African-American congregations is forcing leaders to adapt their leadership styles to fit the present landscape. This willingness to consider a new approach will go a long way toward making it happen successfully.

Leaders must also deal with other questions:

- "Do you think you can muster the patience to tolerate a more affluent people?"
- "Do you think you can face with a spirit of humility people who may be more educated than in times past?
- "Can you without pressure or prejudice treat as colleagues those individuals who desire to express their sincere feelings about the mission, vision, and values of the church?"
- "Do you think you can answer the demands of today's congregant?"

Even when church leaders answer these questions affirmatively, it is imperative to acknowledge the need for training and continuing education, using as their theological basis 1 Timothy 4:6-16, as the writer gives instruction to the person responsible for assuring order and orthodoxy in the church.

Take pains with these things; be absorbed in them, so that your progress will be evident to all. Pay close attention to yourself and to your teaching; persevere in these things, for as you do this you will ensure salvation both for yourself and for those who hear you. (1 Timothy 4:15-16)

This passage suggests the idea that the pastor needs to engage in a personal regimen of spiritual training and continual internal development. Today's congregants demand a level of excellence and biblical accuracy benefiting the person as a church member and as an individual believer. For church leaders, there is little room for mistakes on their part as they are servants to God's people. I was encouraged throughout the project by the sense of gravity displayed by numerous participants concerning this need.

A theological shift is becoming more evident. The concept of a servant-leader has begun to settle in. It is the belief that fellow church members were not merely servants or people who desired service; instead church members are viewed more often as partners in ministry. The theological implication was clear because it highlighted an idea that people of God are partners together with Christ as revealed by the Apostle Paul: "For we are God's fellow workers; you are God's field, God's building." (1 Corinthians 3:9)

This is a concept that is still required, but the idea that church members are beginning to view one another as partners in ministry, including leaders, is encouraging. The advantage for the church is found in the desire for people to find encouragement, camaraderie, and strength in an environment which promotes collegiality and cooperation. The church will benefit from this shift, and the Black Church as an institution will thrive amid a changing identity.

IMPLICATIONS FOR THE PRACTICE OF MINISTRY

One of the strengths of the research is the fact that it included people from a wide variety of geographic, economic, and cultural backgrounds. Representatives of various regions brought a variety of experiences and ideas, which helped create a unique perspective. The project proved there is a need to lead pastors and laity in a process of training which would facilitate exploration of a variety of existing leadership models. Virtually every one of the participants indicated they were not aware of the existence of the named leadership models, which include (a) Authoritarian (Autocratic), (b) Consultative, (c) Participative, (d) Visionary, (e) Supportive and (f) Hands-Off (Laissez-faire).

Young people who aspire to serve in the local church, the African-American church specifically, are the individuals who will benefit the most from training opportunities involving the six leadership modalities. They need to learn the importance of the application of each model. Opportunities for role play based upon a variety of scenarios may help them to understand one model could not be used in every circumstance. Students of the leadership modalities would realize the Westermann model and concept of using the six modalities along a continuum would prove to be most helpful.

An advantage of training young people aspiring to be leaders in the church the six modalities is the possibility of setting the stage for long-term implications in leadership styles well beyond the twenty-first century. Young people can be instrumental in the formation of new leadership paradigms.

Implications for future use of the project model among gender specific groups would be helpful in the creation of collegial partnerships among men and women involved in ministry. It is apparent that men and women have different ideas about which leadership modalities are more beneficial than others. It would be a helpful training activity to survey the root causes behind the negative connotations one leadership style communicates in relation to another. In other words, why do people avoid specific models of leadership and why do they prefer others? Is it all a matter of experience and training, or does individual personality play a role? This information will be valuable in helping future leaders learn flexibility.

The implications for future opportunities to develop working relationships which cross gender lines would help to promote the mission of the church. Women and men serving in lead roles would gain an appreciation for the models as they learn to move from one modality to another based upon certain learned sensitivities and given situations in ministry.

The use of the diverse models of leadership was prevalent based upon geographic locations; for example, rural versus urban, and urban versus suburban. Those participants who lived in rural areas were more likely to practice one particular mode of leadership as opposed to another; that was participative. Individuals serving in rural areas benefited from the participative model because more responsibility was placed with the laity due to the frequent absence of professional clergy. The pastor in the urban church was in many cases the person who set the full agenda of the church and expected the entire congregation to follow. The rural church was the opposite; the life of the church depended upon the people who lived in the immediate area. Therefore, if the minister was not present on a given Sunday, the laity was charged with continuing the ministries and mission of the church until the preacher was scheduled to return.

It is often up to the lead male (Deacon Chair) or female (Church Mother) who serve as the cohesive element in the church. It would benefit many urban and suburban pastors to gain an understanding of the methods of leadership that allowed many of these churches to remain thriving institutions regardless of the number of people who attend the church.

It is important that this training in the various modes of leadership involve pastors and laity both. Many church leaders have expressed interest in learning more about their changing constituency, while some have voiced their belief people have not changed, others are facing reality. The failure to pursue other courses of leadership will lead to the death of long-standing Black Churches.

The data reveals what many have speculated regarding the shifts of ideology and practice within the African-American community. The Black clergy and church leaders are obligated to respond. It is essential for the African-American church leader to begin the process of developing a strategy of reclaiming lost souls for Christ. The tragedy is that many are still not aware of this information that directly affects their ministry. Continuing education on this subject will benefit the entire church, regardless of ethnicity and historic origin.

SUGGESTIONS FOR FUTURE RESEARCH

Future research should be conducted on the evolution of leadership motifs that involve the growing idea of partnering in ministry. The Pauline epistles would be a good starting point for the formation of a Biblical Theological Foundation emphasizing real partnerships (Romans 16, Philippians 4, 1 Corinthians 3). As individuals become more aware of their role as co-laborers in the faith, more attention must be given to the positive aspects of cross-cultural partnerships, men and women, and adults serving with youth. The church continues to struggle with issues of people working together as partners in ministry. Issues such as collegiality, equality, and overcoming racial, ethnic, and gender barriers for the greater causes of doing ministry should be addressed in the project.

In conclusion, discovering pastoral leadership models for the 21st century becomes essential for the body of

Christ. All churches, despite their racial-ethnic composition, must continue to investigate and act upon the slow deterioration of their congregations. Church institutions can no longer rely on the moral compass of society to lead individuals through the doors. The obligation to seek the salvation of the people in surrounding communities is on the church universal. Change begins with the people who are in positions of power. Time is no longer on the side of the church.

APPENDIX

DESCRIPTION OF THE PROJECT

The qualitative research method involved a series of interviews with pastors and laity from selected regions throughout Texas. Each of the interview sessions served as opportunities to receive information from the indigenous local church lay leaders who provided data for the proposed research activity. The research activity led to equipping sessions which helped the researcher to inform participants of the results from the study. Moreover, the researcher gained additional information for formulating viable conclusions regarding the discovery and use of a variety of leadership models.

Quantitative research methods were employed in the pursuit of data which would either prove or disprove that shifts in demographics, the rise in affluence, and the increase in educational opportunities has affected the mindset of the African-American church member.

The research methodology included both qualitative and quantitative research activities, along with a case study approach to attain information. Research instruments included interviews with pastors and laity, the use of two questionnaires; one for clergy (Appendix A) and one for laity (Appendix B). Interviews with pastors were conducted prior to the conferences and seminars to set a foundation for the research and add a broad-based perspective on the subject of leadership. As a result of the interviews and prior study, a PowerPoint presentation (Appendix C) was developed and used as a catalyst to prompt discussion on the subject.

A session evaluation instrument (Appendix I) was also used to evaluate the process and the sessions.

The examination of Pastoral Leadership Models for the 21st Century Church required several procedures to answer the five research questions guiding the focus of the project. This section discusses the procedures used to conduct the project in four parts: General overview, meetings, research questions, and other procedures.

OVERVIEW

Associate ministers and laity were enlisted in Texas to engage in a two-hour information gathering and listening activity which helped to formulate the initial premise for my research. Laity persons, sensitive to leadership issues, were enlisted along with associate ministers who had not served as senior pastors. The group was charged to consider six specific leadership models and styles and critically consider six specific leadership models and styles. The models include, (a) Authoritarian, (b) Consultative, (c) Participative, (d) Visionary, (e) Supportive and (f) Hands-Off (Laissez-faire).

The next step included interview sessions, questionnaires, and material for pastors and laity. Each participant was asked to identify their style or mode of leadership and identify a model of leadership from their past. Participants were asked to explain their rationale for utilizing one form of leadership over another. After the process of identifying a particular style or combination of leadership modalities, participants were asked to critique the results of the given mode of leadership and access how he or she will lead in the future.

The third step required group participation in an Equipper's Conference, which is a combination of information acquisition and sharing, offered to a mixture of laity and pastors. The conference involved the sharing of preliminary research findings which included a historic explanation concerning the "Rise of the African-American Preacher" and the rationale behind his historical status in the Black Church. Respondents also received an overview of the research findings on the demographic shifts among the African-American community. The class participants were encouraged to offer insight on the possible implications of the research data for their present ministry assignment.

The fourth step involved two evaluation sessions; both sessions were scheduled for two hours in duration. One session included participants from the Texas Women's Missionary Union Sisters Who Care Conference, and another session included clergy leaders. The group evaluated the demographic findings, possible intra- cultural implications upon the African-American church, and offered for record their feedback and suggestions for use of the results of the research findings.

Five meetings were held in addition to the interviews and additional research conducted to examine pastoral leadership models. The five meetings included church leaders and laity from all over Texas. Each session was designed to include church leaders and laity from rural, urban, and suburban churches, as well as churches with small to mega size memberships. The following report vignettes are the detailed descriptions of the conference meetings held to conduct the research.

RESEARCH QUESTIONS

The following procedures were adhered to in order to address the five research questions which guided the project:

Research Question 1: What leadership models are appropriate for the 21st-century African-American church? A review of the literature regarding leadership models for the 21st century was conducted. Interviews with pastors and laity were conducted to determine current leadership models being used in their church. Questionnaires were also used to gather data regarding familiarity with leadership models and leadership preferences. Respondents were also challenged to critique the styles of leadership in which they were most familiar and explain how it affected their area of ministry. The critique was to include the socio-economic status of their congregation, along with the average level of education of the church members.

Research Question 2: What, if any differences, exist in the leadership model preferences between rural, urban, and suburban churches? Several meetings were held to address research question two. Participants from rural, urban, and suburban churches were included in all meetings and interviews. Input included both laity and clergy from each of these communities. The mixed clergy and lay composition of the focus group participants, along with the regional diversity built into the project, were key to providing the data needed for the inquiry.

Research Question 3: What degree of relevance exists for the authoritative leadership model in the 21st century? This problem/question required a look at what is currently being done in churches and how useful/effective the authoritative mode has been. Participation of laity and clergy in group meetings included interview questions, *PowerPoint* presentations for clarity, questionnaires, and statistical data, all of which were used to address this issue.

Research Question 4: What is the role of the laity in the African-American church in regard to their place as both leaders and partners? Laity was provided an individual questionnaire which addressed their perceived role in the church. Church leaders were also asked to address their perception of the laity's role in the church. The two groups were provided the opportunity to discuss their thoughts on their roles in joint sessions as well as on the evaluation.

Research Question 5: What cultural and ideological shifts exist that may have affected the mindset of the African-American church congregant? A review of the literature regarding cultural and ideological shifts was conducted. Statistics regarding demographic shifts and leadership models were presented using a PowerPoint presentation. Questionnaires and discussion groups also addressed this issue.

Pastors Interview Questionnaire

Please write your responses to the following questions. Responses will also be shared verbally during the group discussion and form the basis for segments of the final project report. Please provide a detailed response to each question.

How would you characterize your style of leadership?

Please specify the person or persons that you identify as your leadership role models.

Discuss your reasons for choosing each individual and highlight the positive and negative characteristics of each. The examples may be biblical or otherwise.

Upon which theological premise or model would you base your style of leadership. Please supply your biblical reference (i.e. 1 Pet. 5:1-4).

What are three main goals or objectives of your present leadership model?

What are the advantages and disadvantages of your present leadership style?

Please discuss three or more major leadership lessons that you have learned as a Senior Pastor of a predominately African-American Baptist Church.

Please express commonly observed mistakes or miscues that you have witnessed in Pastor-Congregant relational matters.

Explain, if any, the change in the African-American mindset toward the following:

(a)   The Church:

(b)   Church Leadership:

(c)   Church Programming:

(d)   The Role of Clergy:

What models of leadership are you most familiar?

Describe the ideal modern day Pastor-Leader. (a) Authoritarian (b) Consultative (c) Participative (d) Visionary (e) Supportive (f) Hands-Off

Names will be kept in strict confidence. You will have opportunity to review the report content and findings prior to the submission of the report to the doctoral committee.

Focus Group Questions

Associate Ministers, Laity and Lay Leaders

Please write your responses to the following questions. Responses will also be shared verbally during the group discussion and form the basis for segments of the final project report. Please provide a detailed response to each question.

Describe the style of church leadership you remember during your youth and young adult years.

What form of leadership styles were you more likely to respond positively to during your early church experience?

Describe the shift, if any, in your mindset that caused you to respond differently to traditional styles of leadership.

What are the leadership characteristics, functions, or styles that caused you to respond positively to the ministry of Christian service?

What key changes in your environment impacted your response to traditional leadership models?

From your perspective, what are the most important needs for the present day African-American Church Leader?

What process should a church leader pursue when seeking to make key decisions affecting the church body in general?

Provide your definition of the ideal church leader.

Provide your definition of the ideal congregant.

Describe those necessities essential for a good church membership experience.

What factors attracted you to your present place of Christian service?

How important is the leadership ability of the pastor in determining your length of service or willingness to unite with a given congregation/church?

Names will be kept in strict confidence to insure confidentiality.

You will have opportunity to review the report content and findings prior to the submission of the report to the doctoral committee.

SUMMARY OF DEMOGRAPHIC FINDINGS

The Dallas Morning News reported in a recent series of articles the statistical data that upheld the stated hypothesis offered in the introduction. The research revealed the demographic shift taking place both nationally and statewide (Texas) of affluent college educated African-Americans to suburban communities. In the Dallas/Fort Worth Area alone the increase in affluent Africa American residents from 1990 to 2000 was a remarkable 205% overall, according 2000 U.S. Census data. According to a June 26, 2005 report (based on a May 2004 study), the Brookings Institution of Washington D.C. cited the movement of Blacks from urban areas to the suburbs in North Texas is second only to that of Atlanta Georgia. Dr. John Logan a professor of sociology at brown university remarked that the demographic shift of African-Americans is similar to that of Anglos that migrated from metropolitan areas in the 1950's and 60's (June 26, 2005).

The suburban city with the highest growth rate is Frisco that grew 29.4% in the number of affluent ($100,000.00 per year income) new African-American families. Followed by the cities of Farmers Branch 24.5%, North Richland Hills at 19.3%, The Colony with an increase of 18.9% followed closely by Coppell at 18.8% and the city of Mansfield with an increase of 17.8%.

The shift from urban to suburban neighborhoods reveals a marked increase in income above the national average of $41,994.00 to well over $100,000.00 per household per year (2000 U.S. Census Data). The increased income or affluence is reported to foster other demands that may prove challenging for traditional leadership models.

For example, one article in the series entitled, "Mayberry-like city puts out neighborhood welcome mat," highlighted diversity as one of the main attractions for one of the families interviewed. The person interviewed referred to the importance of her children living in a racially diverse neighborhood as a major factor in her choice of homes. She inferred in the interview that her major concern was the well-being of her children in regard to their skills and abilities in the area of socialization (*Dallas Morning News;* Sunday June 26th).

In another article the respondent remarked that he enjoyed the peace of the suburbs, but also felt the need to serve those individuals who were less fortunate than he is. He communicated the need to "give back" to young people by providing summer jobs to low income youth as a means of service to his old inner city roots. Many of the people interviewed throughout the course of the news series displayed a sense of debt to the people from the poorer inner city communities in which they recalled their own years of nurture. Those individuals that have "left" the inner city continue to feel a sense of connection and the need to help others gradually immerse from the depths of despair and poverty. It is important to mention that others who were interviewed throughout the series expressed a sense of isolation from their community (African-American), one respondent found his sense of belonging within the confines of his predominantly African-American church congregation.

An important lesson learned by this student based upon the statistical data and reports from the articles in the study was that this new group of congregants will demand a new type leader. Leaders will be challenged to equip and inspire individuals who have chosen the suburbs as a refuge and display a spirit of social action and a drive toward community empowerment. Pastors faced with this kind of high spirited constituency will be challenged to allow such individuals to utilize their creative juices for bold community initiatives. The clergy or lay leader who is uncomfortable coaching people with this high-energy level will risk losing this talent base to a congregation that embraces this kind of enthusiasm and social vigor.

Comments from Participants

PASTOR

I operate out of this one because my group is young and they need a whole lot of guidance. I think that when we grow we can come to learn about this model and I can hear from the people and we can be on one accord. I like this, but we are not there yet. I do think that there are times when people have ideas about things and you see what they will accomplish. In order for us to do a great work at our church, I do know that we have to do a better job at letting people know what God has placed in our spirit so that the work of God can go forward.

I believe that right now, this being done in some form at my church right now. I do get excited when young people come up with ideas and they are encouraged to try them. From where I sit, I know that this may useful in some places, but this is not at all one that I choose to try.

LAYPERSON

I do think that people should follow the instructions of the pastor. I also think that there are times when meetings are unnecessary, you just have to make decisions and go on. When we talk about things, people do feel like they are a part of the plan and they are more than likely to do what is needed. At least they (people) feel like you hear them. I am used to this form of leadership because as a small child, this is the one I remember being practiced the most. Our church was "in the country" and we did not meet but two times a month with our pastor, so we had the grown folks ran the church and they all had to agree. Every church will benefit from a pastor who helps to lay the course of direction for the congregation. People will have a better idea of what they are doing when they know the vision. They can also operate with a goal in mind and be quick to serve without somebody always looking over their shoulder. As long as they know what to do, they will take the initiative to do what needs to be done. The church that has support from the man at the top usually does better, because it means that we are all on the same page. The more we see this the better off we all are in the long run.

I don't see anything wrong with trying this if the people do two things: (a) Pray first (b) And every now and then let the pastor know what's going on.

Layperson

As a BSM Director I know that there are times when you cannot allow well-meaning college students to make certain types of decisions. I do think that someone has to take the stance for certain things and be the authoritative voice. This form of leadership is good as you attempt to train young to become leaders. I believe that when we do this, we allow them to give input and also learn from you at the same time. I practice this form of leadership most often because you want the students to own the ministry of the BSM. To own something, you need to do more than just hear what "I" the "Director" thinks, you want to know what student thinks from their level of under-standing. I think that when this style of leadership is practiced we are helping people to better understand the "Big Picture" and we are empowering them to do the work on their own. This helps young people to grow. I find myself in this mode of service most often and the students know that I am there to help them go wherever they need to go within reason.

There are times when we need to serve in this capacity especially when you are working with college students because both and them need to know when to allow them to spread their wings.

Pastor

I do believe that there is a shift in the culture. We need to learn what these young people are doing and thinking so that we can minister to them. The problem with "Black People" who have money is that they don't know what to do with what they have. They don't know how to invest and surely they don't know how to support the church. I live and pastor in the rural, I can attest to the fact that a lot of "people of quality" leave the area after they graduate from high school. What I struggle with is helping those who are left behind. I have learned that many of them don't have the highest ambitions, especially if they are young. Leaders have to work hard at figuring out who these people are. We find ourselves working harder to relate, especially when you don't have much help. We have to try other things, that's just the way that is, we can't keep doing things the "same ole way."

Layperson

People sure are changing, and they don't think are act the way in which they use to years ago. It is true that nothing stays the same.

We have people who are doing better financially, I think that they need training as well in this area. We have been blessed in that people who have died in our church, have left money so that the ministry can go forward. I know that has not always been the case at our church.

People don't move in droves to where we are, they do come, but not like they do in other areas. We are like Rev. Johnson's group, a lot of the people who stay behind just choose not to do "big things" so we have to work with the people God sends us. The leaders have to determine where the people are, in the mind. They have to build a program or ministry that will meet the people and fulfill their needs. We cannot stop our mission of saving souls, no matter where people come from or who chooses to stay. Leaders surely are going to have to learn how to do more than just one thing. The people will make sure that this is the case.

LAYPERSON

I can tell you that there is a culture shift, you didn't have to look much beyond the college campus. We will be called upon to deal with the issue of males and females, the growing acceptance of "alternative lifestyles." We know what the bible says about the matters, but we still are going to be called upon to deal with each of these matters. People need to understand that the future has arrived to the present. More and more young people are coming to college campus, especially young women, they are coming in pursuit of better lives. I suspect that they will always seek out some of the same things for their new families. I have discovered that they simply need guidance, we can give that to them if we but recognize them. A great number of young people are moving from

the Urban areas but still a great number of the more educated students are moving back into the downtown areas
of major cities for the same reasons as whites. I think that
we need to prepare to deal with people no matter where
they live.

Leaders today are challenged to learn the language of
the people they are called to serve. For example, if God
moves a person to serve in a given area, that person like
any foreign missionary is going to be called upon to learn
the interest, the social stresses and story of those people.
I see no difference for those leaders called to serve in our
everyday environment.

Leaders need to maintain both an "open mind" and
an "open heart." I cannot down play the importance of
training—training—training.

PASTOR

Authoritarian and Supportive are the models that I
use most often. I do that because the congregation that I
pastor is a young and unlearned group of people. As they
advance in training, I give them leadership positions and
support them in their role.

The role model that I chose to follow was the leadership style of my late pastor, Dr. Z. Broadus. Dr. Broadus was a visionary, a teacher, leader and supporter and
a coach. He believed in Christian Education. He would
sometimes override the church decision because he
was able to see the problems ahead or in the future. The

character in the bible that I model myself after is Nehemiah because he was a builder and a leader; also, Jesus. The Leadership style of Jesus taught me not to be a dogmatic traditionalist, but to be godly in what I do. I have become all things to all men that I might save some (gain) some. What leaders need today are Education, Identification, character traits, influence and knowledge of the needs of humanity and a vision. I have learned that we must guide and not drive the people teach and not punish the people. When preachers drive or mistreat the people, this is a big mistake and it turns people off. We have to get where the people and then we can lead them. (9) I am most familiar with the "Authoritarian" style of leadership.

LAYPERSON

I came up under participative pastor. We had church only 2 Sundays a month. Wed. night prayer meeting and teacher meeting. We had Sunday School every morning. We respond to the pastor of the church whatever the style of leadership. I learned that for the church to grow, you must always be supportive especially when you see thing moving in a positive way.

If things are moving in the right direction, I tend to go along with what the pastor as the leader says. If things don't go right I believe that we should discuss and come to an agreement on our direction and plan. When things go well, I feel good and go with the leader, that makes me respond in a positive manner. I saw how my pastor left the running of the church up to the people and how the people worked with him keep things moving, that was participative and it worked for us and it can work today. Training. The leader needs to pray and then check with the pastor before a move is made. One who follows God and one who can work with the people.   A   person who can follow leadership and trust that God is leading the leader. People need to be together. People trying to do something.

Layperson

Participative: Pastor Carter was an intinerate pastor, he served more than one church and was with us one Sunday out of the month. Yet the church was open 3 days per week: Wed. night, Saturday and Sunday. He trained and empowered church leaders to serve.

I do better with the "Participative and Supportive." For me, the traditional models were the two that I mentioned. I do not respond well to authoritative leadership if it is the only style used because I believe that I have something to offer and contribute. When people can demonstrate the fact that God speaks to them as well as others it gives you the opportunity to serve and grow in God. My children were adults and I was in the midst of a transition much like a change in season in my life. I felt the call to work with students and God opened doors that allowed me to do just that and it got even better when he supplied a pay check. All leaders need to be trained and take every opportunity to receive training in an ever-changing world. Seek the opinion and sentiments of the people. One who is in constant contact with God. One who is willing to serve beyond any perceived boundaries. A person must have a shared vision and be willing to serve. The chance to serve and affect positive change in the lives of young people.

PASTOR

My group is young but they do not respond to this form of leadership very well. I don't like it myself because it is "old school" and it tends to cause the leaders to look down on people.

I do believe in talking to the people and getting ideas from them. Even if I am going to make a decision, I like to know what others think about it.

I think that this is a good way to lead because people get involved in the process and they can take ownership of the program.

I like to think of myself as a visionary because the things that we do are "out of the box" people in my church know that our goal is to save the souls of the younger generation. I think this is a good thing to do but due to the age of our congregation, we have not reached this point, but I do think it's a good form of leadership.

I can't see myself doing this too often because I want to pretty much be involved in all of the "goings on" in our ministry area.

PASTOR

I tend to believe that there are times when a pastor has to simply make a decision. You don't have time always to call meetings and see what others think.

I do bounce ideas and things of this nature off of people and I do want to know what people think. I must say, that if I think that the choices of the matter are coming from God, despite our objections or the "naysayers" I will go forward. I think that this works with a mature congregation who understands the vision of the pastor. I honestly like when people take the reins and get things done. If we are together, then there is no problem with this form of leadership. We built our church on this premise, "God told me to build a church and I laid out the vision and God made it happen. I think that it was this form of leadership that allowed to walk into our building debt free. I feel like I am a coach and a guide to our people even now. People have to learn how to grow into their own; I think that is one of the services of the "Shepherd." I am sure that there is a time and place for this type of leadership style, I won't knock it for others, but I want to be kept in the loop about most things that happen around the church.

PASTOR

I know that there are times when you can't wait on the crowd, you just have to keep moving. I try to keep people informed about the things that I do and attempt to solicit information from people so that they can help to inform whatever decision I am about to make.

This is really my most dominant style of leadership. I realized a long time ago that you need to get the people involved in things at the front end of a project. People who are a part of the actual planning will come to own the thing. This is a good form of leadership and one that I practice as well, we are an ethnically diverse rural congregation, we have grown because people have gotten the vision and they run forward no matter what. The people have come to believe in the program of the church. I have no problem standing in the background; as a matter of fact I really prefer it. I think that it helps people when they know they have someone they can consult with on a daily basis or "as needed" basis. I think that more of that needs to take place.

There are times when we as pastors have to trust that God works through people out of the presence of the pastor.

Pastor

I am very familiar with this style of leadership, but I do not believe that it should be the predominant style from which people should operate from. I think people are different today and they don't response to dictatorial stances like they did in the past. As a leader, I prefer to talk with others about the decisions that I make. I think that it is also good to have other people on your side when the time comes to make crucial decisions that will affect your ministry.

Ministry is all about giving other people the opportunity to serve. Who knows what God is attempting to do in a person's life. I challenge pastors to invite people into service and see the benefits of the request. My father was a pastor and this is the kind of pastor that he was, visionary. Dad believed in laying the idea out of the table and watching him and others bringing the dream to fruition. This form of leadership helps people know that God sends the vision and the people are responsible to make the vision or the dream come true.

A pastor or church leader should always be in the posture of a mentor, coach or guide. We are called upon to "equip the saints" for ministry so that they can build up or edify God's Kingdom. There are absolutely times when people should be trusted to do those things that will benefit the church, people need to be reminded that the church does not belong to the pastor, it belongs to God and all of us are servants.

Pastor

Our church caters to another generational group because of this fact. We do things that other pastors don't necessarily agree with, like "Gospel Rap," but that's what works for us. I know that nowadays people don't simply accept the answers that you give to them because they can now go and get the information for themselves, so the younger generation is more educated. Young people don't know what to do with the money they have. For my people, they don't have much, but they need education in what to do with what they have.

Lubbock is growing, but the people I serve have to be taught that the world is bigger than their neighborhood. I believe that as leaders we need to get out of the old tradition, especially if it is keeping us from reaching people. We need to think of new ways of doing things. We better find out what works for where we are or we will be "by ourselves."

PASTOR

I can tell that people are different but they will work with you if they believe that you as the leader know where you are going. People are smarter, maybe too smart for their own good; it keeps some people away from the church because they think that they have all of the answers until the "bottom falls out." Our people obviously have more; I don't think they know what to do with it. Where I serve, our greatest test is helping the young people gain they hope they need to get out of these ruts that they place themselves into. As leaders, we have to prepare ourselves for all of these different people and the different ideas that they have about doing things.

We definitely need to know how to use more than one method of leadership. We really need to know how to use all of these and more.

Pastor

I do think that there is a shift in the culture and people are not moved by some of the things that they used to be moved by. Our emotions and even worship is changing. I agree that people have more "book sense" but they have less "biblical sense" and seemingly less common sense.

If our people learn the importance of pooling their resources they will learn the true power and worth of their affluence.

Even in West Texas we see that more people are moving to the city, I am dealing with a people who prefer a peaceful and quiet life over traffic and the fuss of the city. Leaders will be smart to expose themselves to new things, ideas and training so that they can either "grow with the people" or simply "grow the people." The smart leader will learn the importance of using all of the methods, not just one or two.

Pastor

The culture of African-Americans we are serving today has truly shifted. We don't even (act) the way that we did in the past. Most have their own agendas and ideas about living life. Their outlook of the church is vastly different from their parents and surely their grandparents.

The rise in education has affected the way that people look at the church and has influenced what some are looking to "get out of the church." I think that

African-Americans know that they are better off financially than in the past, but the tragedy is the amount ignorance regarding what they can do with what they have.

We are seeing a shift away from the rural and urban areas and those pastors who live in those declining communities have to decide whether they are going to leave or stay. If they remain behind, they better have a plan for survival.

Today's leader in order to survive must shift the way they guide God's people. In order to survive, leaders are going to do well if they remain on the "cutting edge" regarding the latest strategies for reaching this new group of African-Americans they are faced with. Leadership methods should be practiced along the type of continuum that was discussed. We cannot continue working out of one tired old method. "Dictators Fall!"

Pastor

Participatory: My leadership style is "out of the box." I am a Pastor of today's world. I am focused on generation x. This generation needs someone they can relate to and God has made it possible. Not holding to tradition by looking to tomorrow. Jesus Christ is my "role model." Jesus accepted everyone with agape love. He sat with the sinners and showed His love for all, and He died and has risen again to complete the work He came to do. Mark 7:5-16 is my theological premise and style of leadership. My first goal is being the type of leader I see in Jesus.

Secondly, accepting and receiving those whom God deems to be saved no matter who or where they come from. Third, not only talking the talk but walking in Jesus footsteps and reaching the so called "unreachable" generation. Fourth, I believe that we must take the church to the unchurched. Advantages of my present leadership: 1) I am a young Pastor who has been where the youth of today are. 2) I have two teenage girls that I can relate to and get feedback from. 3) God has given me the knack for reaching the youth of today. Disadvantages Include: 1) Traditional Pastors and church are disapproved of my methods. 2) The negative feedback from the older generation. 3) Lack of sufficient funding (when you don't do it the way others want you to do it, then they don't want to help you as much.)

One leadership lesson is to allow God to lead me, so that I will know how to lead others. 2) Be a true leader and not be led by those in the church. 3) Stay true to what I believe in no matter what others may say or think.

Mistakes in Pastor-Congregational Relations: (A) thinking numbers mean everything. (B) Too many anniversaries and meaningless programs (Pastor and Wife Anniversary) we put too much emphasis on things like this and not enough on kingdom work. (c) Not enough of discipling new converts. (d) Letting the congregation dictate to them how to run the church. A) The church has become about the buildings and not about the people. B) Church Leaders, they are not being properly trained for the work involved. (C)Church Programming places too much emphasis in the wrong programs (anniversaries) not mission minded. (D) Role of the Clergy looks like they follow the people and not leading the people anymore. Worry about numbers and not about souls. The model of leadership I am most familiar with. (1) The best again is Jesus. The worst model of leadership is one who is lazy and who will not be about kingdom work. The modern-day Pastor-Leader 1) Is the one who cares for the People. 2) Numbers aren't everything 3) One who has a passion for saving should. 4) Who can relate to the world we are in. 5) One who is not afraid to get their hands dirty. 6) One who is not afraid of making a decision without the people's approval as he is being led by God.

Pastor

By living and example of Christ, and love God and love humanity. My pastor and my teaching from my grandparents. A humble prayerful shepherd knowing God. To spread love everywhere I go and starting new churches and supporting them. Advantages are being observant of the sheep and keeping God's will in my work.

I have learned to stay away from: A) Secular media. B) Secular and Political Leaders C) Contemporary Trends. Not enough ones, as in Acts 2 about the state of doing the same thing. I go back to what is projected by mass secular media. The media has messed up the minds of people. Servitude as Christ is and was as in the washing of the disciples' feet. The ideal leaders are those who follow the bible. The problem is that some look more at what is popular and entertaining.

Pastor

As that of a servant-leader Previous pastor M.D. Smith. My ultimate example is Jesus Christ. 1) To lead the lost to Christ. 2) To have a spiritually healthy church 3) Be an example by showing love to all. No answer. No answer. Pastors tend to "beat the members across the head with the scriptures and this is not a good thing." No answer. No answer. A good model is the pastor who could pull the people together and treat them all the same!

Pastor

The need to utilize this form of leadership is needful in my case because the people tend not work without direct commands from the pastor. I think that this is a good concept; I would like to grow to this point in my East Texas congregation. I do solicit the thoughts of others when I am thinking of new ideas that may benefit the entire church. I think that this is an ideal, but I do not see this happening as of yet in my present setting. I want to be able to point people in a certain direction and watch them grow and make the project or program happen. However, I am somewhat frustrated over the fact that so many tend not to have the desire to do much of anything. The leadership that is needed in our church is best served by a person who can give clear direction regarding the "what it takes" to do things in our church. This style of leadership is a good thing to talk about, but the people have to be willing to follow through. "I cannot see this happening where I serve at all. I need to say at least at this present time, not now."

LAYPERSON

The people who are subjected to this form of leadership usually have their growth stunted and are not free think. I do appreciate it when pastor includes the congregation in his line of thinking about things. I would like to see more proactive thinking from the membership as a whole. I do see where this can still allow people to be apathetic and less apt to think on their own accord. I do not think that this is idealistic if you give the people an opportunity to think. I must admit that because I serve in the prison system, that this is not the way that we make decisions, they are made on the basis of the "authoritarian" model, we do however believe that this is the best way to lead in a parish setting. People who operate using this model tend to have more ownership. I always wanted to see this type of leadership style work, especially at the church we once served. The people were so negative until they did not have much initiative to do anything; we did more of the work that was warranted. If we can learn that people are more intelligent that we think things can get done with good results. One must agree that people

must be will participants and have a heart for their local church. I think that motivated people who are on the
same wavelength of the pastor as it concerns his overall vision for the church can operate in this area and do
well. I think this is possible because the leadership and
the people have the same goals for mission and ministry
in mind.

Layperson

As a lay person, I think that what works best is when
people are given opportunities to think for themselves. I
guess that there are times when you need to make the
decisions from the top, but I don't think this has to be the
case always.

I think this is a good form of leadership because it at
least allows people to offer their opinion on matters of
importance. I think it also shows that the pastor is trying
to open the door for input.

This is the model that I function best in myself. Even
as a kid I saw this kind of leadership model practiced
within our church because the pastor was not always
able to be present every Sunday. One thing that we did
have was Sunday School every week. The people decided
the course of operation for the church.

I think that if the pastor offered many of us this kind of
support, we would do a good job is serving and not let the
ministry down. Many people, if they risk to live the vision
rather than simply dream. A leader described under this

form has to trust the people he is work with so that they can feel free to serve without any hindrances from him. They need to know that the project really belongs to each of them and they have the freedom to do the work.

I could see this working with people who come up with ideas independent of the pastor and the pastor trusts them to do a good quality job without any fear that they would do something against the teachings of the church.

PASTOR

The Black Church was led by male pastors at the time because it did serve as second family for most. The model was that of a family and in East Texas where I serve, it continues to be that way in many cases. Pastors now must recognize that this increase in the education of the people causes them to ask more questions about everything the leader is attempting to do. I also notice that the people are demanding more from the church, but they are not necessarily willing to do more themselves. Black people might be making the money but we sure do not see it in our church. We find ourselves constantly asking almost to the point of begging people to give to those things that they know we need in our church. Don't mention staff...

My area tends to be more stagnant. Most of the people living in my area are individuals who are "stuck" or they are simply satisfied with their plight in life. I think that is what affects our church, "they just don't want to do anything." The hardest thing for me is to get over my frustration of not moving forward. I am tired of begging people to do those things needed for us to survive. As a leader, I have to seek more patience and find new ways to move my group in the right direction.

I have discovered that we don't have to work out of just one model of leadership. We do better to work using all of the ones presented at those times when the situation arises for that to take place.

LAYPERSON

I can understand the rise of the Black Pastor as a male because that was the way things were at the time. I must stay that I also know that as a female, men continue to apprehensive about accepting me because I am a female, but I must serve because I too am called to ministry, not the pastorate but I am a minister.

Churches must now deal with the rise in the education of women, especially in the area of theology. Men who are leaders are going to have to accept the role of women in the church and give them a place of service or they will find other places even other denominations from which to serve God and be recognized.

People have more money, but they need to be taught what they need to do with it and as church leaders we need to help them know what we are going to do with their dollars. We will find that if we do not respond in this area, the people will go to those churches, maybe even "white churches" where they can see their dollars at work or at least working for them. We can tell that people are moving around and relocating. I think that people are trying to move to better their condition. We must meet them with new styles of leadership and help them get what they are searching for in these new places.

I have talked about the merits of using other models of leadership. The truth is, I think in most settings one has to use or work along a continuum of models when you are the lead. I must admit that in my setting in the "Prison System" I do not have the option always to do so, I am forced to set the program and make sure that others follow my lead or the lead of my husband. I do think that the best thing to do is to use a variety of the models presented. One model of use is not good enough or realistic.

LAYPERSON

I am not a minister but I agree that things are the way they are because of the end of slavery and the need to set a structure in the new Black community in the south.

It is becoming obvious that the more people learn the more they want from the church, especially young people. We are going to be pressed to learn their language and learn what their needs are and how we can reach them where they are. I know that people have more money, knowing what to do with the money is another story. Our (Af. Am.) priorities seem to be different for some reason.

Where I am, the people are moving in and out. I do think that we need to be ready to offer them what they need for however long they will be in our area. Leaders are going to be challenged to find out what the needs of the people are as they constantly change. The reality for us as leaders is understanding that if we don't change, we might find ourselves out of a church or in a "know win" situation.

Pastor

My group is so small, and many of them are so young, I have to be the person who is making the majority of the decisions. I do believe in talking to the adults around me about the ideas, hopes and dreams that I have for the ministry. I want them to be a part of this new birth (new church plant) experience. I think that this is a good way to lead because it helps people to get involved in the process. I am having trouble with people understanding my vision for our young church. I think that as I improve in this area, we can better empower people to do things with our ultimate goals in mind for our ministry. I think this is a good thing to practice once the people mature to the point of doing things on their own. I look forward to serving as the "coach." Right now, I need to be coached. I can see myself doing this as people grow in ministry. I have no problems in offering my blessings to those who have ideas for the ministry to run do them, especially if it is for the greater good of the work.

Pastor

I tend to be "out spoken" and direct. The people I pastor need this kind of leadership because many of them are former "addicts" and we need a lot of structure where I am from and have to be tough in my delivery. I am trying to build a group of men who I can talk too about ideas that "God has given" me so that they can own the ideas and see that the needs are met for our congregation. I think that the more committed our people become, the more I look forward to them carrying the baton and getting things done. While I admit that my style of leadership is primarily "authoritarian" I realize that in order for me to be a more effective leader, I am going to have to shift more responsibility into the hands of the people or we will not survive. I think that failure to do so will "kill the pastor, literally." I came to the area with a vision of starting a church and we are well on our way. I do believe that I am sharing the ultimate vision for our church with the people and we are moving in the right direction. It is slowly progressing forward but I do see growth, especially when people take the initiative to do things without me asking.

I feel like I am coaching our men and my wife is coaching the women. We like this model because it shows us that the people are growing. They are more apt to do things on their own and I like to see that. I have no problems in this area because it shows me that the people are growing.

LAYPERSON

I think there is a time and a season for all things. There are times when you have to give directions without meeting with a whole group of people.

It's always a good thing when you can talk too and listen to your pastor regarding matters of ministry. I think that when you hear from him his direction on things, you can offer your input and pray that God is guiding you in your thoughts as well, especially if your advice or your views is being solicited.

This gives people an opportunity to share their gifts and do those things that are needful for the on-going work of "The Kingdom." It is always a good thing to know the direction of the "Man of God" and do operate within those "bottom line" parameters. It is good to have a good idea of where that person is coming from and you can see if that overall vision fits what you think may the plan that God has for your own individual walk in life. I think that it is good to have a leader, in particular your pastor as a coach. It is good because you get the opportunity to serve at the same time, you have the freedom to do those things that needed with just enough lee-way to test the ministry waters around you. People who understand the vision can be trusted to do things on their own because they know where the church is going and what the ultimate goals and objectives for the church are in the given community.

LAYPERSON

I think that there are times when direction must be given without consulting whole groups of people. When decisions must be made on the fly, leaders should understand that there are appropriate times to make those decisions. Input from other people is a good thing and should be sought. I think that when a person hopes to have individuals working with them in reaching a common goal, you do well to respect their input. To allow another individual the freedom to move within the bounds of ministry knowing that they can bring new ideas to the forefront is a good thing. People tend to grow when they can be creative.

The bible is clear, "people parish because of the absence of a vision." It is good to know the direction of the church and the ministry so that you can know and work within those boundaries seeking an agreed upon outcome How can people really grow if they are not being mentored or coached by someone? The leader who participates in this form of leadership is helping their ministry team to become more effective. One would think that leaders would welcome this form of leadership because if there should come a time when key leaders are not present for consultation, the organizations must function without harboring the fear that they cannot move without the blessing of the "higher-ups." It is a good practice to utilize this method so that when those days come and the leader is nowhere around, the people are not stymied, but feel the freedom to complete certain task, knowing that whatever decisions they make will suffice.

PASTOR

It is true, things are not like they use to be. The size of my congregation calls for me to set up my church much like they did back in the day when the pastor was the "Father Figure."

I have acknowledged that there has been an increase in education and I try to keep myself is somebody's class all the time and do the same with leaders in our church. We need to get where the people are. People might have more money, but I am confused about ways to get them to spend their money with the church in mind. The people are coming to our neighborhood and I am already attending city meetings to find out what is coming to our area so that I can have something to offer them. I think that it is bad planning to attempt to decide what the needs of people are once they arrive. "While you are trying to figure what people need, they will get impatient and leave." I see that we have to make adjustments. Ministers need not let too many training opportunities pass them by. I know that I must change and I must learn to all of the models presented. I take these opportunities to look at myself and make corrections when correction is needed.

It is best that I learn to do more than just one style of leadership.

Pastor

I am the "Father Figure" in my church. My wife is the "Mother" and my two children are very involved in the church; so in that manner things have not changed for us. I think that people with the different professional skills cause us to rethink the way we communicate to them, I discovered that I have to answer questions about my ministry, when years ago a "Church was a Church." Now people want to know about your programs and everything.

Other might have more money, but the people I serve, don't have much money. I know this because, we feed many of them and attempt to offer them services that will help them get on their feet after a life full of bad decisions.

We have a serious challenge where we are, because the area started out as a "forgotten area" in the rural, but now new homes are sprouting up every day. Our new challenge is trying to get ready for this whole new group of people who are coming. They live in houses that are 300 to 400k. "This ain't the group I have right now."

We need to see the hand writing on the wall and do what it takes to meet the needs of the people. We need to do things that we may not be used to doing, that is, attend Chamber Meetings and meet City Officials. We need to also know the direction of the municipality in which we are located. All this is new but it is needed. I know that if our church is going to grow I need to know when the best time is for me to use each of these models.

LAYPERSON

I think that the size of the church kind of dictates the way that you set up your ministry. I don't think that you want it to stay that way. I think that it is a good thing that people are more educated. We have to educate ourselves and remain "fresh."

The facts are clear, but the question is, "What are people doing with their money?' Our people (African-American) are more prone to spend their money on something material than spiritual. We are living in an area that is "pregnant with potential" and we must take the steps needed in training and leadership development and program planning that will meet their needs now. We also do well to study demographic reports to see what type people are coming to the area. The people are expecting the leadership to be ready. We cannot say that we are not aware of the movement of people to the area because we are a part of that shift ourselves. Training is the key. I think that we all agree that we need to learn how to use each of the leadership models at the appropriate time.

LAYPERSON

Size of the work does matter. You would think that as you grow, you can begin to do things differently. Education is fine, we still have the "Word" and we are responsible to deliver that word. We are responsible no matter how much education they have, theologically or otherwise. People have money, but they need to be taught.

We know that the people are coming to the south, just look at the neighborhoods sprouting up around us. If we plan to receive them and have those things in place that will "hook" them, then we will be fine, cannot wait for them to arrive. Today is not even the same as yesterday. We are challenged to meeting the needs of the people are we fade in the back drop. One model is not sufficient; we need to learn all of the models of leadership so that we can do them all when the time is right.

Bibliography

Actemeier, P.J. 1 Peter: *Hermeneia*. Minneapolis: Fortress, 1996.

Agria, Mary A., and L. Shannon Jung. *Rural Congregational Studies: A Guide for Good Shepherds*. Nashville: Abingdon Press, 1997.

Akin, Daniel L. and Rainer, Thom S. *Vibrant Church: Becoming a Healthy Church In the 21st Century*. Nashville, TN: Life Way Church Resources, 2008.

Akuchie, Ndubuisi B. *The Servants and the Superstars:* "An Examination of Servant Leadership in Light of Matthew 20:20-28," *Christian Education Journal* 14 no. 1 (Autumn 1993): 43.

Anderson, Leith. *A Church for the 21st Century: Bringing Change to Your Church to Meet the Challenges of Society*. Minneapolis: Bethany House Publishers, 1992.

Barna, George and Jackson, Harry R. *High Impact African-American churches: Leadership Concepts from Dome of Today's Most Effective Churches.* Ventura, CA: Regal Books from Gospel Light, 2004.

Boice, James. *The Gospel of John 18:1-21:25.* Vol. 5 Grand Rapids: Zondervan Publishing House, 1979.

Bolman, Lee G., and Terrence E. Deal. *Leading with Soul: An Uncommon Journey of Spirit.* San Francisco: Jossey-Bass Publishers,1995.

Boyd, Gregory A. *God at War: The Bible and Spiritual Conflict.* Downers Grove: Inter Varsity Press, 1997.

Bramson, Robert M. *Coping with Difficult People.* Garden City: Anchor Press/Doubleday,1981.

Bridges, Darrell Bridges. *A Model for Utilizing Evaluative Instruments in The Developing of Leaders in a Young Church.* Portland: Theological Research Exchange Network, 1995.

Broadus, John A. *Commentary on Matthew.* Grand Rapids: Kregal Publication,

Buttrick, David. *A Captive Voice: The Liberation of Preaching.* Louisville: Westminster John Knox Press, 1994.

Carter, James E. and Trull, Joe E. *Ministerial Ethics: Moral Formation for Church Leaders.* Grand Rapids: Baker Academic, 2004.

Campbell, Robert C. "Executive Advice: Remarks by Senior Church Leaders." *Christian Century* (March 1993): 321.

Cedar, Paul A. *Strength in Servant Leadership.* Waco: Word Books, 1987.

Chapell, Bryan, and Hughes Kent. *1 & 2 Timothy and Titus.* Wheaton: Crossway Books, 2000.

Collins, Jim. *Good to Great: Why Some Companies Make the Leap and Others Don't.* Harper-Collins Publishers, 2001.

Cone, James. *God of the Oppressed.* New York: Maryknoll, 1997.

Conger, Jay Alden. *Spirit at Work: Discovering the Spirituality in Leadership.* San Francisco: Jossey-Bass, 1994.

Cottrell, David. *Leadership Biblically Speaking—The Power of Principle-Based Leadership. Dallas: CornerStone Leadership.* Dallas: Cornerstone Leadership, 1998.

Cranfield, C.E.B. *The First Epistle of Peter.* London: SCM Press, 1950.

Dale, Robert D. *Good News from Great Leaders: Leadership and Conflict.* New York: The Alban Institute, 1992.

Davies, W. D. and Dale C. Allison. *A Critical and Exegetical Commentary on the Gospel According to Saint Matthew.* London, New York: T&T Clark International, 2004.

Douglas, Lloyd C. *The Minister's Everyday Life*. New York: Charles Scribner's Sons, 1926.

Electronic Resource, *Leadership in the 21st Century*: Center for The Development of Evangelical Leadership. Charlotte: Gordon-Conwell Theological Seminary, 2001.

Elmore, Tim. *Authentic Influence: Leading Without Titles*. Nashville: Lifeway Press, 2001.

Exell, Joseph S. *The Biblical Illustrator*. New York: Fleming H. Revell Company, 1849.

Fairbairn, Patrick. *Ezekiel, and the Book of His Prophecy*. Minneapolis: Klock and Klock Christian Publishers. 1979.

Finzel, Hans. *The Top Ten Mistakes Leaders Make*. Cook Communications Ministries. 1994.

Fluker, Walter E. *The Stones that the Builders Rejected: The Development of Ethical Leadership from the Black Church* Tradition. Harrisburg, Pennsylvania. 2002.

Frazier, Franklin E. *The Negro Church in America*. New York: Schocken Books, 1963.

Frazier, Franklin E. *The Negro Church in America:* C. Eric Lincoln, *The Black Church Since Frazier*. New York: Schocken Books, 1975.

Freedman, David Noel. *The Anchor Bible Dictionary*. New York: Doubleday, 1996, c1992.

Garland, David E. *Reading Matthew: A Literary and Theological Commentary of the First Gospel*. New York: Crossroad Publishing Co., 1993.

Greenleaf, Robert. *Servant Leadership: A Journey into the Nature of Legitimate Power and Greatness*. New York: Paulist Press. 1977.

Greenleaf, Robert. *Servant Leadership: A Journey into the Nature of Legitimate Power and Greatness*. New York/Mahwah: Paulist Press. 1991.

Greer, Eugene E. Jr., *Baptist: History, Distinctive, Relationships*. Dallas, TX: Baptist General Convention of Texas, 1996.

Hagner, Donald A. *Word Biblical Commentary 33B: Matthew 14-28*. Dallas: Word, Incorporated, 2002.

Halverstadt, Hugh F. *Managing Church Conflict*. Louisville: Westminster/John Knox Press, 1991.

Hare, Douglas R.A. *Interpretation-Matthew*. Louisville: John Knox Press, 1993.

Hendriksen, William. *Commentary on 1 & 2 Timothy and Titus*. London: The Banner of Truth Trust, 1959.

Heuser, Roger, and Norman Shawchuck. *Leading the Congregation: Caring for Yourself while Serving the People*. Nashville: Abingdon Press,1993.

Hicks, Beecher H. *Preaching through a Storm.* Grand Rapids: Zondervan Publishing House, 1987.

Higginson, Richard. *Transforming Leadership: A Christian Approach to Management.* London; 1996.

Hinson, Glenn E. *Spiritual Preparation for Christian Leadership.* Nashville: Upper Room, 1999.

Howse, W. L., and W.O. Thomason. *A Church Organized and Functioning.* Nashville: Covington Press, 1963.

Ironside, A. H. *Expository Notes on The Gospel of Matthew.* London: Pickering and Inglis LTD, 1948.

Jennings, Ken, and John Stahl-Wert. *The Serving Leader.* San Francisco: Berrett-Koehler Publishers, Inc., 2003.

Karris, R.J. *The Pastorals.* NTM. Wilmington: Michael Glazier. 1979.

Keck, Leander E. *The Church Confident.* Nashville: Abingdon Press. 1993.

Keener, Craig S. *A Commentary on the Gospel of Matthew.* Grand Rapids: William B. Eerdmans Publishing Company, 1999.

Keener, Craig S. *A Commentary of the Gospel of Matthew.* The IVP New Testament Commentary Series 1. Downers Grove, IL: InterVarsity Press, 1997.

Kesner, J.W. *The Prophecy of Ezekiel*. Bogard Press, Texarkana, TX. 1968.

Kittel, Gerhard, Gerhard Friedrich, and Geoffery William Bromiley, *Theological Dictionary of the New Testament*. Grand Rapids, MI: W.B. Eerdmans, 1995.

La Flure, Jennifer. "A New Face of Affluence: Black Wealth in Suburbs". *Dallas Morning News*, June 26, 2005.

Lincoln, Eric C. and Lawrence H. Mamiya. *The Black Church in the African-American Experience*. Durham, North Carolina: Duke University Press. 1990.

Lincoln, Eric C. *The Black Church Since Frazier*. New York: Schocken Books, 1974.

Lincoln, Eric C. *The Black Church in the African-American Experience*. North Carolina: Duke University Press, 1991.

LaRue, Cleophus J. *Power in the Pulpit: How America's Most Effective Black Preachers Prepare Their Sermons*. Louisville: Westminister John Knox Press, 2002.

Lea, Thomas D., and Vaugh Curtis. *Bible Study Commentary:1 & 2 Peter, Jude*. Zondervan Publishing House, 1988.

Leas, Speed B., and Roy M. Oswald. *The Inviting Church: A Study of New Member Assimilation*. New York: The Alban Institute, 1987.

MacArthur, John, Jr. *The MacArthur New Testament Commentary: Matthew 16-23*. Chicago: The Moody Bible Institute of Chicago, 1988.

Mc Cormick, Blaine and David Davenport, *Shepherding Leadership: Wisdom for Leaders from Psalms 23*. San Francisco, CA: Jossey-Bass, 2003.

Marshall, I. Howard and Philip H. Towner. *A Critical and Exegetical Commentary on the Pastoral Epistles.* London, New York: T&T Clark International, 2004.

Messer, Donald E. *Contemporary Images of Christian Ministry*. Nashville: Abingdon Press, 1989.

Miller, Michael. *Kingdom Leadership: A Call to Christ-Centered Leadership*. Nashville: Convention Press, 1996.

Minear, Paul S. *Commands of Christ*. Nashville: Abingdon Press, 1972.

Mounce, William D. *Word Biblical Commentary: Pastoral Epistles*. 46. Dallas: Word, Incorporated, 2002.

New American Standard Bible: 1995 Update. LaHabra, CA: The Lockman Foundation, 1995.

Nouwen, Henri J. *In the name of Jesus: Reflections on Christian Leadership*. New York: Crossroad Publishing Company, 1989.

Overberg, Paul. "Minority Groups Breaking Patterns". *USA Today*, August 2005.

Plummer, Alfred. *An Exegetical Commentary on the Gospel According to St. Matthew*. London: Robert Scott, 1911.

Ramsey, Michaels, J. *Word Biblical Commentary: 1 Peter*. 49. Dallas: Word, Incorporated, 2002.

Rediger, Lloyd G. *Clergy Killers: Guidance for Pastors and Congregations under Attack*. Louisville: 1997.

Raboteau, Albert J. *Slave Religion: The "Invisible Institution" in the Antebellum South*. Oxford Press, 1980.

Schweizer, E. *The Good News According to Matthew*. Richmond: John Knox, 1975.

Shawchuck, Norman, and Roger Heuser. *Leading the Congregation—Caring for Yourself while Serving the People*. Nashville: Abingdon Press, 1993.

Sims, Bennett J. Servanthood: *Leadership for The Third Millennium*. Cambridge: Cowley Publications, 1997.

Skinner, Tom. *A Renewed Black Leadership*. New York: Tom Skinner Assoc., 1981.

Simmons, Charitey. *Leaders for Black Churches*. Christian Century (February 1995): 101-102.

Stahl-wert, John and Ken Jennings. *The Serving Leader: 5 Powerful Actions That Will Transform Your Team, Your Business and Your Community*. San Francisco: Berrett-Koehler Publishers Inc., 2003.

Stott, John, *Basic Christian Leadership: Biblical Models of Church, Gospel, and Ministry*. Downers Grove: Inter Varsity Press, 2002.

Swamidoss, A. W. "Diakonia as Servanthood in the Synoptics." *Indian Journal of Theology* 32 no.1-2. (January-June1983): 30-39.

The Holy Bible: King James Version.

The Holy Bible: New Revised Standard Version. Nashville: Thomas Nelson Publishers, 1989.

Tichy, Noel M. *The Leadership Engine—How Winning Companies Build Leaders at Every Level.* With the collaboration of Eli Cohen. New York: Harper Collins Publishers, Inc., 1997.

Tidwell, Charles A. *Church Administration: Effective Leadership for Ministry*. Nashville: Broadman Press, 1995.

Wachtel, Paul L. "The Poverty of Affluence: A Psychological Portrait of the American Way of Life." *Psychology 6*, no.4 (December 1985) :753-754.

Ward, Ronald A. *Commentary on 1 & 2 Timothy and Titus.* Waco: Word Books, 1974.

Washington, James Melvin. *Frustrated Fellowship: The Black Quest for Social Power*. Raleigh, North Carolina. 1990.

Westermann, John J. *The Leadership Continuum: Authoritarian, Consultative, Participative, Visionary, Supportive, Hands-Off Biblical Model for Effective Leading*. Deer Lodge: Lighthouse Publishing. 1997.

White, John. *Excellence in Leadership: Reaching Goals with Prayer, Courage and Determination*. Downers Grove, Illinois: Intervarsity Press, 1986.

CPSIA information can be obtained
at www.ICGtesting.com
Printed in the USA
FFHW010315010419
51321226-56830FF